Violence
and
Theology

HORIZONS IN THEOLOGY

Violence and Theology

CHERYL A. KIRK-DUGGAN

Abingdon Press
Nashville

VIOLENCE AND THEOLOGY

Copyright © 2006 by Cheryl A. Kirk-Duggan

All rights reserved.

This book is printed on acid-free paper.

Library of Congress Cataloging-in-Publication Data
Kirk-Duggan, Cheryl A.
    Violence and theology / Cheryl A. Kirk-Duggan.
        p. cm.—(Horizons in theology)
    Includes bibliographical references.
    ISBN 0-687-33433-0 (paperback : alk. paper)
    1. Violence--Religious aspects.   I. Title.
BL65.V55K57 2006
201'.76332--dc22
                                                                    2006028579

06 07 08 09 10 11 12 13 14 15—10 9 8 7 6 5 4 3 2 1

MANUFACTURED IN THE UNITED STATES OF AMERICA

CONTENTS

INTRODUCTION

There was a time when many of us thought of violence only in terms of other people's lives, of what happened on the six o'clock evening news. Even growing up with my dad, the first African American Deputy Sheriff in the State of Louisiana since Reconstruction, was more about the importance of embodying and advocating for justice than the acts of violence that necessitated his job. He never had to fire his gun during twenty-seven years on the force. Yet, with the terrorism of September 11 those of us privileged to live in these United States realized we were no longer so safe. Violence also struck when Katrina landed on the Gulf Coast, destroying lives and wreaking havoc on the ecosystem, buildings, and grounds. Like many others, I was stunned and grief-stricken by the depths of loss and the violence resulting from systemic oppression in the aftermath. September 11 and Katrina exemplify two different types of violence, one orchestrated by human beings, one triggered by nature and exacerbated by blatant disregard and incompetence.

People in the West, including Christians, are not exempt from violence. History, popular culture, natural disasters, and religion indicate as much. The development of civilization emerges through war and conquest. Often those persons who had already acquired some things, *the haves*, decided to become elitist, *the have-mores*. The development of the United States included the stealing of lands from Native persons, the massacre and enslavement of thousands of them, and the warehousing of those who remain in modern slavery on reservations. That development included persons of African descent being bought and sold into inhumane, chattel slavery; a slavery that was crucial to the growth of colonial, Southern aristocracy. Many times people constructed their philosophies and reasons for engaging in such violence as an act of faith or a dictate of manifest destiny. Despite what recent events might suggest, violence is not a new challenge to culture or faith. Violence did not emerge with the advent of punk rock, rap, hip-hop, and video games. Violence has been a part of Western history since before the beginning of recorded history. Violence is so present that we often do not see it, for we have become immune; it is everywhere: from prison systems to cartoons, from gang wars to triumphalist Christian hymns; from opera to domestic squabbles. Matters of culture, faith, and violence, which beg the question about the relationship between violence and theology, are played out in a myriad of ways, in both popular and classical culture.

Much of what has happened in history gets replicated in art and remnants of social engagement. Popular and classical culture, from rap, television, and video games to Shakespeare, Greek tragedies, Grimm's fairy tales, and opera contain plot after plot riddled with violence: wars, massacres, murders, homicide-suicides, assault, rape, manipulation, humiliation, destruction, and annihilation through the use of words. Several popular, often acceptable, and sometimes economically viable forms of violence involve activity ranging from sports, religion, and sex trafficking to state-ordered murder. Organized professional and amateur sports, especially hockey, boxing, lacrosse, and football, all involve controlled rule-limited aggression.

The driving questions for this volume are two: What is violence? What is the connection between violence and theology? In a post-September 11, post-Vietnam, and post-Holocaust world, it is crucial for us to ask these two questions. Before providing a working definition of violence and before ascribing any ideas about the connection between violence and theology, it is essential to note the caveats that frame these two questions. First, there are no easy answers and this volume does not simplify or justify the complex variations of violence that exist throughout the world in secular and sacred cultures. Second, there are various schools of thought as to why people do bad things and how God responds in the midst. Most of these theories are incomplete, passé, or unsatisfying at the level of experience. Third, the notion of divine judgment itself involves violence, a concept often uncomfortable and difficult for believers to grasp, especially when someone they love or they themselves are on the receiving end. Fourth, people tend to view violence, such as a state-ordered death penalty and war, differently from cases where a mentally ill parent murders a child. Thus, in religion and in life, there are times when we legally justify violence.

Some would argue that violence is always morally wrong, regardless of the circumstances. Others would claim that violence used to protect others is justified and morally sound. Some see violence on a continuum from the acceptable to the never allowable. As this volume unfolds, violence—that which causes harm—will be defined and explored in religious and cultural settings. Particularly, we will explore the connections between the capacity and activity of causing harm and the discipline and embodied reality of theology; that is, how one talks about and understands the reality, nature, and person of God, and how that God and humanity relate. Theology is a component of religious expression.

Religion, particularly Christianity, in its texts, development, and belief systems, involves numerous acts of violence, which many consider good: creation comes out of chaos; Abraham acquiesces to murder Isaac as an act of obedience; and the doctrine of salvation may include a concept of atonement, which in a loving God demands the death of the son to appease the wrongdoings of humanity. Many consider other types of religious violence bad: the Romans crucify Jesus; St. Paul persecuted Christians; so-called orthodoxy martyred so-called heretics. In more recent history, terrorists assassinated Archbishop Oscar Romero while he consecrated the Eucharist, March 1980; theologians continue to use the language of "just war" to legitimate casualties ["collateral damage"] of war. Men and women ordained to preach the word and break the bread have slandered their vows through acts of pedophilia and molestation; some people of faith sit on juries and vote for the death penalty, while others could never condone the death penalty, even when the convicted party is a serial killer and has committed the most heinous of crimes.

Faithful or not, we cannot escape the reality and impact of violence in our world. Adult male and female school teachers have slept with underage students placed in their care. Daily, children are kidnapped and sold into sexual trafficking; many people become refugees because in the land of their birth, they are persecuted because of what they look like or because of what they believe. In some countries where one family/one child is the law, infant girls are left on garbage dumps and trash heaps because the family desires a boy child. In a quest for support and family, many young people join gangs and have to murder another human being as a rite of initiation. Some college students participate in hazing where they do harm to others as a similar form of initiation for fraternity or sorority membership. The ban on assault weapons has been lifted in the United States, and nation-states around the world continue to jockey to have access to nuclear weapons so they can develop a credible nuclear threat to those who already possess nuclear missiles. Some executives do harm that destroys people's livelihoods and life savings, violating trust by so-called white-collar crime. In pursuit of the almighty dollar and power, some people lie in such egregious ways that they cause harm: public trust is compromised; some lies result in oppression or death of others. What does this human capacity to engage in the mutual destruction of others say about faith, about human reality, and about our relationship to God?

Violence and Theology explores the pervasiveness of violence in society and in Christian thought and life from an interdisciplinary perspective. An interdisciplinary perspective, one that includes ideas and concepts from two or more academic subjects or fields of study, is essential to help us explore the many different contexts in which violence emerges in our lives and in the lives of our neighbors. Such an approach helps us both identify and think theologically about many kinds of violence that surround us, including the violence in a basic foundational text like the Bible, where violence may be up front and center, but due to our earlier training we are blind to the depth and impact of that violence. *Violence and*

Theology is an extended essay that: (1) explores the landscape or general dynamics of violence and posits a Womanist theological-ethical perspective as a critical analytical tool; (2) does theological reflection with various selected narratives that privilege violence: the Bible, literature, television, Grimm's fairy tales, and video games; and (3) analyzes selected traditional categories of systematic theology: salvation, Christology, and theodicy. Systematic theology is a way of talking about God, where what theories and doctrine in one area of thought say about God cannot contradict anything in another area. For example, if God (theology) is trinitarian, then one cannot say that the Holy Spirit (pneumatology) does not exist or is irrelevant to the nature of God. If the church (ecclesiology) is the body of Christ (Christology), then the church must practice love of neighbor as embodied by Christ. Salvation is a term that frames one's understanding of liberation or freedom in relationship with Christ Jesus. Christology studies the dynamic life, witness, and ministry of Jesus; *Theodicy* is a term coined by Leibniz to talk about divine justice in light of the contradiction between God's attributes and the problem of evil in the world.

Violence and Theology is both testimony and treatise: a witness of my observances of the impact of violence on our lives as religious beings and an exposition, based upon personal observation. *Violence and Theology* is an invitation for you, the reader, to become more cognizant of the many iterations of violence in your lives, with the hope that awareness can lead to acceptance of the reality of this violence and action on your part to help transform the violence.

> *Violence, violence all around:*
> *Humpty, Dumpty fell; Jack broke his crown.*
> *Someone lied, someone committed homicide.*
> *Lucy forever clobbers Charlie Brown.*
> *Wile E. Coyote in his obsessive fanaticism to overcome another*
> *Continuously causes himself harm;*
> *Lady Macbeth spiraled down.*
> *Lots of Mad Hatters running round,*
> *Violence, violence, violence abounds:*
> *Do you see it?*[1]

CHAPTER ONE

LANDSCAPE OF VIOLENCE

Globally, violence is a major health epidemic: more than 1.6 million people die each year due to violence. Yet, many acts of violence go unreported. Further, millions more are injured and suffer egregious mental health, physical, psychological, and reproductive health problems due to violence. Violence, a complex, cyclical problem, shapes our families and communities. Many perpetrators have a faith practice, with an underlying theology. Violence is theological, personal and communal, external and internal. Silence is often a culprit. Statistically, youth violence has increased, and most violence to women includes sexual abuse. Often children suffer along with their mothers, and abuse to the elderly remains the most hidden form of abuse. We have a lot to atone for, to achieve prevention and holistic health.[1] Before we can atone, we must identify the problem.

Why does any human being need to violate the person of another human being? Is this compulsion more about a lack of self-esteem and self-worth that needs to control others; is this about an abuse of power? To understand the actuality of violence and theology, how they connect with people's lives, we explore violence; that is, this section provides a working definition of violence and excavates forms of systemic violence more pervasive in United States culture than we like to admit, particularly because we think of this country as the "land of the free and the home of the brave." We even codify this sentiment in our pledge of allegiance: "One nation under God, indivisible, with liberty and justice for all." Freedom does not come without cost, and bravery may not be all that it is set out to be.

WHAT IS VIOLENCE?

Violence is that which harms. Violence can be blatant or subtle forms of aggression, hostility, cruelty, brutality, force, and the harsh wielding or misuse of power. Power is the capacity to be in a position of authority, or to have a position of strength to influence, control, or impose one's will on other persons, processes, institutions, and systems, with or without their resistance. Such a misuse of power unfolds through individual and communal behavior. At the level of community, violence can be systemic, where laws, rules, and legislative or bureaucratic bodies are intentional about keeping tight reins on those deemed *other*. The experience of violence is universal and complex. For some, violence is anything that hurts another sentient being or anything in creation. Violence may represent an infringement on human rights and the rights of creation. This dehumanizing action is intrusive, and it destroys creativity and one's inner essence as it disallows one's freedom. There are so many, almost mind-boggling levels of violence: the implied and actual; psychological, emotional, physical, mental, and spiritual; economic, religious, cultural; racial, sexual, verbal, and attitudinal—all of which are relational.

Violence is relational because it affects our entire way of being: whatever is meaningful, loving, and important to our vitality. To relate is to connect. Our earliest connections are through family systems. Family relationships affect all other relationships; we imitate behavior mirrored before us. Families and others who have an impact on our lives help us define what is meaningful, significant, and important. Within intimate relationships, we learn to love and hate. Karen Baker-Fletcher notes that our world contains hatred and unnecessary violence, or traumatically destructive action.

Given that "creatures eat other creatures, whether plant, animal, insects . . . we all participate in levels of necessary violence to feed and sustain our physical lives. A certain degree of destruction is part of the cycle of life."[2] Our concern is unnecessary violence.

Acts of unnecessary violence involve more than the perpetrator and victim(s); they include their intended and unintended consequences, which affect individuals, communities, and systems. Systemic violence can occur because enough individuals and collectives or institutions made up of like-minded individuals embrace the beliefs, behaviors, customs, and rituals that support violence. We see such violence in legal, social, business, and religious systems. For example, those convicted of trafficking crack cocaine get a much stiffer prison sentence than those trafficking the same amount of cocaine. People who traffic or use crack cocaine tend to be poor and nonwhite, an instance of systemic legal violence that usurps an individual's rights.

Violence is often self-imposed and can have an inward or outward thrust—sometimes so extremely subtle that litigation would not be feasible. Internalized violence may not be apparent to the individual or to their immediate community; yet it is not any less deadly. People internally self-destruct; they commit slow suicide in many ways: alcoholism, drug abuse, overeating, compulsive spending, gambling, and staying in abusive situations. Violence external to an individual or group can also be subtle. If the violence is embedded in traditions and rituals, perpetrators and victims may not be aware of the ongoing wrongs. Elsewhere, the violence is so heinous, so blatant, it is inconceivable that one human being created by God could inact such acts on another. The horrors of war, sex trafficking, brutal murders, and domestic violence make plain the depths and scandalousness of violence, marked by horrific disregard and disrespect for God-created life.

THEOLOGY AND VIOLENCE

God-talk and how human beings relate to God is the purview of theology. While many people pursue graduate study to hone their skills and understandings as "professional" theologians and scholars, people who have never critically studied theology and religion can be theologians. Theology is the study, contemplation, and conversation about who God is, how who God is relates to who we are, and what we believe because of our understanding of God. When and how we pray and how we live in light of those prayers imply a type of theology. When we take seriously our responsibility or stewardship for how we live in the world, this is theology. Whenever we think or talk about the impact God has on the world and our lives, we are doing theology. All religions that focus on a God, particularly the three Abrahamic religions (Judaism, Christianity, and Islam) have a theology or set of beliefs and related praxis or ethics; that is, a set of doctrines or practices regarding how we ought to live our lives. Theology, however, is not stodgy and irrelevant. For Christians, theology is not just what the particular denominations say about who God is and how we ought to live in relation, theology pertains to how we embrace various belief systems as incarnated in Jesus the Christ, and how we then embrace Christ as model, for the church is the body of Christ.

Some people see themselves as more spiritual than religious, which begs the question "Can one have a theology related to spirituality for those who do not embrace formal, organized religion?" I believe the answer is yes. When one thinks and talks about God and orchestrates one's life around a personal understanding of God, then one experiences theology. We learn from others and construct a theology based upon what makes sense to us. Some people construct their theology focused on personal devotion and piety. Some construct their theology based upon a prescribed system of beliefs from church doctrine or a particular life philosophy. Others construct their theology based upon their understandings of what it means to be a person of faith who must respond to injustice. Latin American liberation theologians argue that God is on the side of the poor and work to change the injustice in their society. Thus, when the *campesinos* have home prayer meetings, they also create co-ops and make sure everyone has electricity.

Theology can help expose the nature and impact of violence on society. For example, Womanist theologians, generally women of the African Diaspora who are scholars of religion, intentionally name violence and oppressions of racism, sexism, and classism—anything that harms people. They do analysis of varied sacred texts, novels, poetry, music, and folk wisdom to name the violence and offer suggestions about how to transform and change this behavior. Womanist thought is theory and praxis, a way of life. Other scholars engaged in liberating God's people understand that anything that obstructs personal or communal well-being and communal development must be examined, and people must be encouraged to believe and act differently.

If we do not address violence, it will not disappear. People who do or cause violent acts usually have a vested interest in continuing their destructive behavior. There is a payoff. That payoff may be monetary, emotional, or social. Sometimes those who do violence have the authority of office or status behind them. Other times people who are oppressed take on the behavior of their oppressors and begin to destroy themselves and others who are most like them.

Theology asks us what it means to be human, what is the nature of society, and pushes us to examine the potential for justice and transformation of violence. Meanwhile, with augmented technology we have the capacity for increased violence with crimes such as identity theft, the disrespect of personal privacy, and more options for creating tools and devices of destruction. Violence places all in a survival mode and diminishes the inherent dignity of the created, denying the *imago Dei* in humanity. Violence displaces the role, holiness, and sacrality of God and of humanity. Violence also blurs the lines of reality and often exudes ambiguity. Sometimes the issues are massive and unwieldy so that it seems violence can never be transformed.

THE SCAPEGOAT THEORY

Scapegoat theory is a helpful theological lens for seeing some of the factors amid the schematics of violence. French literary critic and cultural anthropologist René Girard[3] has a theory about violence used to create and control societies called "scapegoat theory," based on the idea of *mimesis*, or imitation. *Mimesis*, to imitate, is vital for our epistemology, the way we know and learn. With "good" mimesis, one desires to learn something from another. Mimetic intimacy, the resulting process and framework of "good" mimesis, involves nonviolence: imitation without conflict and without sacrifice.[4] Mimetic desire concerns the experience where two or more people (the model and the subject; the latter learns from the former) desire or want or relate to the (object) same person, place, thing, or status. This framework of model, subject, and object is Girard's mimetic triangle, which illustrates his theory. This desire can lead to rivalry: several participants want the same thing, object, or opportunity. Girard suggests that mimetic desire and its resulting ritualized conflict involves the resolving and controlling of the resulting violence, or acquisitive violence. Negative or acquisitive mimesis, where subject and model desire the same object, occurs where the process can engage in rivalrous and destructive activity. Such activity requires a victim, a scapegoat, to allow culture to continue. In various settings, at work or at play, many of us wield power and authority, brilliantly or brutally. We use our power and authority to create a living laboratory of thought, experience, and erudition. Some micromanage, chide, and destroy. The scapegoat becomes the reprobate, which allows satiation of lust and thirst for calm.

Once a scapegoat is identified, the dominant group can release its rage and fear and violent sensibilities, and gain a sense of peaceful community. This shift invokes a sacred structure, rooted in a sacrificial sacred altar, the center of creating and recreating communal, social solidarity. The success of the scapegoating process often turns on the victim's invisibility or on being named and experienced as "other." This naming may help us hide our own collusion in the scapegoating process. In media and texts like opera, film, popular music, Scripture, and novels, we receive warnings about making victims perpetrators and feigning our own innocence. The question before us is how to resolve the conflict.[5]

Those persons deemed "other," because of their embodied differences (gender, race, class, age, or sexual orientation) must be recognizable and vulnerable. Increased violence occurs when one names someone(s) other. Girard names these conflictual rivals as monstrous doubles. Creating differences, or being aware of particular differences, creates a distinct kind of social order. Girard claims that, culturally, human beings imitate the desire of another, because when they come together around the same thing or object, they use one another as models and begin to resemble one another. Unfortunately, this imitation can also produce abnormal greed or acquisitive mimesis. Increased similarities create societal confusion. Ultimately, individuals and groups engage in violence as they struggle to be different. Yet through their struggles they end up looking and acting more and more like one another, and they focus on a person or group of persons who look, behave, or think differently. These kinds of differences often make the person or group of persons vulnerable, and that difference often makes them the target of a particular group's united effort to define themselves and those deemed other, by focusing their own thrust for power against those who cannot react. By psychologically or physically eliminating or purging the ones who are different, a group establishes itself. Lynching, for example, is the classic act of collective violence.[6] This group execution or ritual assumes the victim is guilty and creates the opportunity to kill, without guilt to members of the in-group. Everyone participates, and the execution takes on a festive air.

The Girardian scapegoat mechanism,[7] then, helps us see that mimetic rivalry shapes human behavior, and provides a way to rationalize violence via religious rituals and myth. Scapegoat theory helps us see theologically as we discern how people interact in the context of their faith, as they blame something or someone else for the particular crisis they are facing. People tend not to need a scapegoat when all is going well. Girard argues that the scapegoat mechanism has been exposed and made ineffectual in the Gospels, through the passion and resurrection of Christ: I disagree. Girard claims the scapegoat mechanism works because the scapegoat is hidden, for people do not overtly say a particular person or group is the scapegoat, rather they act that way. If the birth, life, death, resurrection of Christ exposes the scapegoat, then there should be no more violence and no further need for scapegoats. History proves this to not be the case. When we do not or cannot see our own complicity in scapegoating, the problem of violence remains. If we see our complicity, then we can no longer feign ignorance of the victim's innocence[8] and theologically must reflect on diminished right relations.

FORMS OF VIOLENCE

Introduction

The following statistics about violence from the the World Health Organization,[9] are astounding. More than 1.6 million people a year experience violent, preventable deaths globally; 35 people every hour through strife and war; 1,424 people are killed in acts of homicide every day—almost one person per minute. Experts report that millions more suffer in silence as they continue to experience gross neglect and abuse at home, school, work, even in religious or faith communities, where they should be safe.

The report delineates the statistics of violence: many women fall prey to intimate violence, where one in two women murdered are the victims of their husbands and boyfriends or former husbands or boyfriends.

Young people, who often have just begun to grow and think for themselves, are frequent victims of violence. Seven percent of deaths among females and 14 percent of deaths among males, ages 15 to 44, are caused by violence. The World Health Organization reports that "drunkenness is one of the situational factors found to precipitate violence."

Up to 6 percent of the elderly say they have been abused—one of the most hidden faces of violence, according to the document. Roughly every 40 seconds, one person commits suicide. Among those aged 15 to 44, suicide is the fourth leading cause of death. Suicide is the sixth leading cause of disability and ill-health in this age group.

In a fact sheet from the Children's Defense Fund in 2006,[10] figures show that in the United States, more 10- to 19-year-olds die from gunshot wounds than from any other cause except motor vehicle accidents. With children under age 15, the rate of firearms deaths is far higher in the United States than in 25 other industrialized countries combined. In the United States (the report has 2003 figures), gunfire was responsible for the deaths of 2,827 children and teens—1,822 gunfire homicides, 810 suicides, and 195 deaths attributed to an accidental shooting. Three hundred seventy-eight were under age 15, 119 were under age 10, and 56 were under age 5. Every day nearly eight children or teens die from gunfire in America, about one every three hours.

From infancy throughout childhood, children are incredibly vulnerable to abuse and violence, from neglect to death, because they are so dependent on adults for their needs and safety. Globally, the violence includes children being forced to be child soldiers, child prostitutes, and child laborers; they are subject to physical abuse, sexual, psychological, and emotional abuse, and abandonment. More children are orphans, and thus homeless or street children. Too frequently, perpetrators take Jesus' words, "Suffer the children to come unto me" (Mark 10:14 KJV), and then actualize "we will make sure the children suffer." Due to the difficulty of reporting and getting reliable data, many experts hesitate to estimate the number of child victims; and not every region defines abuse in the same manner. Yet, many socioeconomic, political, and technological forces aggravate children's well-being from armed conflict and divorce to lack of potable water and poor educational opportunities.

Some abuse issues, like the ones stated above, are global; others are more regional. In North America, hundreds of children die each year from parental abuse. In Asia, children die from poverty, caste systems, migrations, population growth, and political instabilities. These conditions in addition to lack of access to nutrition, medical care, and educational systems produce conditions of abuse and neglect that result in such things as child soldiers and prostitutes and malnutrition, child marriage, child labor, and discrimination against girls. In Africa, socioeconomic, political, and environmental challenges place children in harm's way of neglect and abuse. There are child soldiers, HIV/AIDS, child prostitution, female genital mutilation, child abduction for sale, premature marriage, physical abuse as discipline, and extended family systems being jeopardized because of urbanization. In parts of Latin America, child abuse and neglect result in physical abuse, corporal punishment, abandoned street children, denial of citizenship. Further, increased Internet child pornography fuels global child abuse and exploitation through prostitution, pornography, sex tourism and trafficking; this vehicle also assists pedophiles in stalking children, across the world. UNICEF notes that the problem is particularly increasing in the United States, and Russia.[11] These statistics indicate that the preponderance of violence makes it a global health epidemic.

Terror and Terrorism

Where were you on the morning of September 11, 2001? A phone call from my sister prompted us to turn on the television and see smoke billowing from one of the twin towers, the immediate aftermath of a plane hitting the building. After 9/11, people in the United States could no longer assume the arrogance of naiveté, assumed innocence, and the promise of safety. President George W. Bush declared a war on terror after 9/11, and with the sanctioning of Congress declared war on Iraq for allegedly having weapons of mass destruction and for being behind the tragedies of that fateful day. That the Central Intelligence Agency (CIA) had reports incredulous of the existence of Iraqi WMDs (weapons of mass destruction), that the primary candidate Osama bin Laden claimed responsibility for 9/11, and that Iraq did not have anything to do with the September 11 terrorist act was insufficient evidence to protect people of Iraq from being harmed and their land defiled. This reality has led to more than 2,500 U.S. military women and men's deaths, numerous civilian deaths, and tens of thousands of Iraqi casualties. These numbers do not even begin to signal the numbers of civilian and military persons that have had amputations, reconstructive surgery, or treatment for post-traumatic stress disorder. That many of these casualties occurred because of suicide bombers who carry their detonators on them changes the dynamics of war—no longer between groups per se, but between individuals who arm themselves out of a zealous, religious, fanatic, ideological commitment: violent acts of theological sabotage. What is this thing called terror?

Violence and terror go hand in hand. Terror is an individual or group tactic of intimidation to effect dread, fear, and panic. Defining terrorism is complex. Terrorism or guerilla warfare is the systematic use of terror, that is, of intense fear, dread, anxiety, and violence, to effect coercion. Not only are the lines between terrorism and organized crime blurred, but the time frame where one explores terrorism affects how one constructs the definition. Intensified nationalism, extremists who amend religious ideology for their fanatical purposes, the correlation between history and contemporary conflict, access to information, and terrorist tactics employed by states shape how one views terrorism. Terrorism as a tool of mass destruction involves chemical, nuclear, and biological warfare and suicide bombers. With terrorism, one makes a theological choice to become creator and arbiter of life and death. Terrorism is an act of violence committed by groups to intimidate a population or government into granting their demands of insurrection and/or revolution, causing intense fear and anxiety.[12] Terrorism, which we can trace to the French Revolution, is intent on producing anxiety and discomfort, often through clandestine activities and meaningful, measurable threats to personal, communal, societal, and political well-being; it is irrational, calculated phenomena bent on paralyzing groups or individuals with fear toward complete control.[13]

Terrorism, then, is a form of violence that often emerges amid colonialism, when three things occur: economic insecurity, militarization, and racism or ethnocentrism. Terrorism tries to erase communal memory, much of which is often controlled by the media. We fail to recognize terrorists because they are just like us—they look normal. Ultimately, every human being has the capacity to do good, and every one of us has the capacity to do evil, sociopaths and psychopaths notwithstanding. Terrorism is not only a matter for the state but also a matter for religion. All religions have engaged in violence and terror; no religion is exempt from this indictment. Terrorism kills the community and creates an ethos of death.[14]

Lee Griffith reminds us that terrorism has an ideology and an anti-theology and ethics that says there is no God, and that practices conquest and ethical dualism, where retribution is the order of the day and the so-called doctrine of deterrence legitimates the use of weapons. One of the fallacies of terrorism is that we can fight it with a war on terror. The U.S. government seems to be addicted to war as a tool of problem solving. In its history, the United States has been a perpetrator of terrorism. Terrorism, the scoundrel that maneuvered these lands from native peoples, that enslaved Africans of the Diaspora, and fought against the Mexicans, has affected nearly every immigrant who has made these shores our home—by desire or by force. War, terrorism, and violence are central to the infrastructure and aegis of the sociocultural and historical ethos of the United States. Ironically, governmental sanctioned terrorism, including war, has taken more lives than so-called terrorists. Terrorism challenges nation-states' monopoly on terrorism. Terrorism, an excuse to heighten a country's militarism with war and militarism, destroys the planet and the poor. Nation-states engage in reciprocal terrorism when they fight a war on terrorism in the name of peace. Violence dubbed a war on terrorism is still violence, which controls emperors, presidents, and thugs alike. Jacques Ellul notes that violence begets violence, and there is no differentiation between violence that enslaves and violence that liberates. The United States is liable for more than seventy different invasions and revolts.[15] Griffith suggests that the antithesis of terror is God; the terror of God is the reality that those who reject all love are forced to endure love.[16] If Griffith is correct, then the heightened militarism of the United States, of any nation-state, cannot but lead to destruction of itself. Given that the Greco-Roman, Persian, Mongolian, Ottoman, and British empires have all perished, this does not bode well for any moves toward U.S. imperialism.

Natural Disasters

Terrorism not only occurs between countries and nation-states, but can also occur with the onslaught of natural disasters. Hurricanes, tsunamis, volcanoes, earthquakes, and floods have created a kind of global terrorism of their own, as most of the continents have experienced tremendous loss of life and devastation to their ecological systems, thus destroying any imagined facades of safety. Some believers come away thinking that natural disasters are some form of punishment from God, as they interpret divinely induced disasters in the Bible. Some people embrace spiritual philosophies or belief systems that may or may not rationalize natural disasters. Sometimes the devastation is a function of a particular meteorological event. Other times, the actual devastation is the result of human error, disregard, and negligence.

* * *

There are other forms of human-induced violence that are not related to weather, but can be equally disturbing, destructive, and demoralizing. Many people experience a kind of terror due to what they look like, their race, social location, gender, or sexual orientation. Such terrorism is a result of racism, classism, and sexism. These forms of violence happen daily, and often go unreported, unacknowledged. People are also terrorized because of their age and their disabilities.

Racism

Racism often surfaces out of ignorant taboos and notions of the exotic, the unattainable, and often the desirable, the "forbidden fruit." An ugly global phenomenon in history and in our present day, racism invades systemic sociocultural, religious, economic, political, and monetary structures rife with oppression, discrimination, injustice, prejudice, and exploitation. Racism is ubiquitous and pervasive. This pathological bigotry is present when: (1) people have limited freedom of choice in movement, work, or residence because of their race; (2) their involvement in the political process is limited; (3) their acquisition of economic power is thwarted because of barriers to educational opportunities; (4) nation-states set policy that depends on the labor of specific racial populations, but deny those same persons equivalent participation in that nation-state; (5) print and popular media denigrate and cause harm to racial/ethnic groups because of the stereotypes they publicize; (6) nations or groups profit from global and geographical structures connected to racist beliefs and actions. Influenced by Western theology, Western culture has posited White supremacist ideology and the superiority of White people over against all other races. Concepts like *the chosen, the elect,* and *People of God,* the misuse of the Genesis texts, the Aryan representation of Jesus, and the privatization of Christianity have excluded and estranged many peoples of color and privileged White races. Racism arises out of historical events. Note that blackness became demonized with Muslims overtaking Edessa, twelfth century; Bubonic or black plague, fourteenth century; African slave trade, fifteenth century, begun in Portugal and sanctioned by the papal bull of Pope Nicholas V, 1454.[17]

Having read about global life experiences and having traveled throughout the United States, in Canada, parts of Central America, Europe, and Asia, I have seen so clearly that racism exists in every culture worldwide, without exception. Some base their concepts of race on religious ideologies, making racism a construct of theology and violence. Others believe that racism is dead and do not realize that not only is racial violence alive and well but Christians used the Bible, which never condemns slavery as intrinsically evil, to justify slavery's existence. Stephen R. Haynes,[18] in *Noah's Curse: The Biblical Justification of American Slavery,* shows how throughout centuries of interpretation, various traditions within Christianity have erroneously identified Ham, son of Noah,

14

as the ancestor of black Africans, and the so-called Noah's curse as biblical justification for American slavery and segregation. Noah did not curse Ham; Noah cursed Canaan, his grandson, the son of Ham (Gen 9:20-27). The roots of racism exist down in the regions within the unconscious, submerged in anger, guilt, shame, and the unknown. Thus racism or racial violence has become normative, commonplace, and results in injustice, which arises amid a distorted distribution of power. We must admit and reject the evil and sin of racial violence, and move toward creating healthier communities and work toward unity as we honor racial differences,[19] along with variation across gender and sexualities.

Sexism

Sexism is the violence of prejudice or discrimination that targets one because of one's gender and sexual orientation. I was not so aware of this type of oppression until I had conversations with women in seminary and heard the stories of abuse and disregard. I heard the stories where daughters were discounted because they were not sons. I know of too many instances where women, had they been men, would have gotten fantastic promotions, high-profile jobs, and significant support. Many women scientists argue that the dearth of women scientists is due to discrimination, not because of some incompetence or lack of intrinsic aptitude. This discrimination is one form of sexism.

Sexism involves the behavior, conditions, attitudes, or values that nurture stereotypes of social roles based on one's sex or gender. Women have been used as nonhuman sex objects, and masculine privilege over women's bodies and their sexuality continues. The myths of male superiority, great sexual prowess, and vanity that justify male pleasure at any cost embody sexism and gender oppression in forms of misogyny and male supremacy. Like racism, sexism occurs across the spectrum of humanity, socioeconomic and cultural arenas; across age, ethnicity, and faith community. Some men exhibit a deeply possessive nature over the women in their lives and see women as objects to own;

thus sexual violence is one means they use to exercise control over them. Some men engage in practices of dehumanization through psychic warping, a mental and emotional dysfunctional behavior. Other male supremacists are incapable of relating to people who are different, and they transfer guilt and responsibility to their victims. Some men take license from the misinterpretation of Scripture to abuse women, and at the least treat them as subservient, rooted in the so-called Fall doctrine and Eve's so-called manipulation of the *adam*, the earth creature, out of whom a bone had been taken to create her. Further discussion on the connection between the Bible and sexism occurs in chapter 2.

Sexual violence in art often imitates that in life. For example, the cinema has gone from covert misogyny or sympathetic indifference to brutality and violent abuse. Contemporary film and pornography not only treat women as objects, including lewd and lascivious poses, but actually depict enactments of rape, and physical, mental, and emotional abuse.[20] Women daily experience violent acts of infanticide, assault, rape, sex trafficking, dowry deaths, and domestic violence, some ending in homicide, in countries developed and undeveloped, rich and poor, during peace and war. Globally, one in every three women has been coerced into having sex, been physically beaten, or been mentally, economically, or psychologically abused sometime in her life. Calculated another way, the United Nations posits that approximately 113 million to 200 million women are missing or dead, from diverse acts of violence: the death of baby girls or female fetuses in countries where the preference is for boy children, domestic violence, and poor medical attention.[21] Sadly, females ages 15-44 are more likely to experience deadly violence or impairment than to experience war, traffic fatalities, malaria, and cancer combined. Every fifth woman on the planet will probably be a rape victim or attempted rape victim during her lifetime.

The high prevalence of HIV/AIDS among women pertains to their inability to garner safe sex and to their inability to escape unwanted sex. Violence is both cause and often consequence of HIV/AIDS—fear of violence keeps many women from help and treatment.[22]

Another form of sexual violence is heterosexism. Heterosexism is discrimination against persons who are gay, lesbian, bisexual, or transgendered. As sexual violence, heterosexism dismisses and devalues homosexuals and contends that such a designation is a lifestyle choice. Homophobia often fuels the discrimination and violence against homosexuals. Oppression, bias, and any psychological, physical, spiritual, or emotional harm done to a person because of gender or sexual identification is sexual violence. The depths of sexual violence span from teasing and stereotypical language about gay persons to a parent saying they would rather their child be dead than gay to hate crimes where a person is murdered because they are gay, lesbian, bisexual, or transgendered. Questions about the dimensions of the human person and about violent acts perpetrated against a person or group because of gender bias are inherently Christian theological issues, when understanding that human beings are created in God's image. Thus, concerns about how people experience their spiritual, emotional, physical selves are ultimately theological questions.

War and Colonialism

Other acts of violence occur amid war and colonialism. Our awareness of war depends a great deal on when we were born, where we live, and our awareness of history. Some people live with the daily onslaught of bombs, tear gas, and bullets whizzing by their ears. War is not a new phenomenon. War, atrocity, or massacre caused the murders of between 180 and 200 million people in the twentieth century, a much larger total than during any other century in human history. Approximately 165 wars or tyrannies in the twentieth century killed in excess of 6,000 people each. Five of these events took more than 6 million lives each. Twenty-one events claimed between 600,000 and 6 million lives each. Sixty-one acts of government-sanctioned violence claimed between 60 and 600 thousand each, and seventy-eight events killed between 6 and 60 thousand each.[23] Many of the worst atrocities occurred in the dark and remain unrecorded. Four to five percent of all human deaths in the twentieth century were intentionally caused by political violence, from terrorist bombings and executed dissidents to battlefield fatalities to starvation among refugees and hard labor in concentration camps.

War is a state of open, declared, armed hostile conflict between states or nations. War involves hostility, conflict, or antagonism, usually as a competition or struggle between opposing forces or for a particular end. There are civil wars (within a nation-state); cold wars (tension over ideological differences that occur via methods of covert military action, with continued though often strained diplomatic relations); and holy wars (war pursued by religious partisans to defend or promulgate their faith). Warfare, organized, structured, extensive, antagonistic conflict between nation-states, organizations, or large groups of people, has involved gross violent, physical force to acquire power, territory, and/or natural resources. War shifted from combat between groups of warriors to including attacking civilians with the bombing of Guernica, April 26, 1937. War often occurs in tandem with colonialism.

Colonialism involves the control by one power over a dependent people or geopolitical area. Colonialism robs the colonized of power, natural resources, freedom, and cultural artifacts that provide one with a sense of purpose: the stories, histories of origins, oral traditions, documents, natural elements, often ritual and traditions—any legacy or heritage they might want to entrust to future generations. Those colonized or oppressed can acquiesce and assimilate. This practice often results in self-denial; or they can embark on self-discovery. The colonized often run into difficulty when trying to affirm the essential realities of pre-colonial traditions and those of the colonizer.[24] The domain of domination for the colonizer is the colony. History records numerous acts of colonialism with war and much destruction. One factor that allows one group to colonize another is that of class distinctions, or classism.

Classism

Classism is the perpetuation and embodiment of fear: fear of difference, fear of the other, fear of lack, fear of powerlessness, fear of losing control. This fear becomes exponential in oppressive political situations steeped in the socioeconomic politics of survival. Control and manipulation of access to education, goods, services, jobs, and the political process involves systemic and intentional violence toward people by virtue of their sociocultural and economic situation.

The term *class* as a social category materialized during the Industrial Revolution era. Prior to the 1770s, the common use of the term *class* pertained to a division or group in schools and colleges. The terms "the poor" or "poor laborers" emerged in the eighteenth century, indicating the relationship between wage earning and poverty. In the early nineteenth century, the phrase "working class" or "classes" emerged to indicate economic process, beyond the earlier implied hierarchy of possessions and social rank. The differentiation in ranks, that is, higher, middle, upper, lower classes, appeared between the 1790s and the 1890s. The late appearance of the term *class* designates the change in attitude toward different social strata and the character of the divisions. Throughout history, the notion of depicting societies as whole groups of people has been prevalent, particularly when explaining or justifying inequities relating to how certain groups of people were treated. When we name the various kinds of oppressions, the "isms," the violence, we do this to expose the wrong and invite you to focus on the opposite of violence; what can bring about transformation, respect, and holistic health for individuals and for society.

The Antithesis of Violence

Justice is the antithesis of violence. Justice is profound, beautiful, relational; the quality of being just, impartial, or fair; the attitude, rule, standard, or ideal of just dealing or right action, particularly as one conforms to this principle or ideal of righteousness; conforming to just law, truth, fact, or reason; to maintain, direct, or manage what is just especially by impartially modifying conflicting claims or the assignment of merited rewards or punishments. Justice intensifies love to honor human relationships and make them more meaningful, and reconciles the relational use of power with the loving gospel of Jesus Christ. Several key thinkers on justice include John Rawls, who sees justice as fairness;[25] Michael Walzer, who sees justice as spheres of justice when dealing with distributive justice;[26] and Robert Nozick, who talks about justice as distribution as long as the distribution occurs through free exchanges by consenting adults, and is made from a just starting position, even if large inequalities emerge from the process.[27] These various views of justice help us grasp the complexity of justice as a response to violence and show there are many options when one works for transformation.

WOMANIST THEOLOGICAL ETHICS

To help us expose violence and realize our own complicity in it, the lens of *Womanist theological ethics* serves as the methodology for this volume. The term *Womanist,* derived by Alice Walker[28] from the term "womanish," refers to women of African descent who are outrageous, audacious, in charge, and responsible. The term refers to a Black feminist who takes seriously the experience of oppression due to class, gender, race, sex, ability, and ecology. To take seriously oppression signals the answer of "No!" to all violence. Walker's definition of *Womanist* is multifaceted and fertile as a foundational rubric for doing critical, creative analysis. Along with the mechanisms of survival, of loving, of taking charge, the term *Womanist* also conveys a vitality of life, a search for knowledge, an embrace of the comedic, the paradox of youthful wisdom, and the capacity to endure amid ambiguity.

Womanist sensibilities celebrate the freedom of being able to love all people and confidently embrace the manifestation of women's culture and life. To be *Womanist* invites balanced, holistic health and loving the spectrum of colors of Blackness. Ultimately, loving Blackness is the capacity to love all people of the African Diaspora and the capacity to love all people, for all other colors together are a part of the color black. *Womanist* theory is also physical, spiritual, emotional, and creative, and evokes a palette of variegated reality, yielding imaginative passion, love, hope, and change. *Womanist* theory, amidst a faith-based curiosity, seeks to discover, analyze, and honor the lives and gifts of the forgotten and the dismissed, of the silenced and the vulnerable.

Womanist theory invites, requires, that one live in present time, while simultaneously being a student of history, engaging in radical listening and discerning, to see, know, challenge, analyze, and make a difference. *Womanist* theory is a field of study and a way of thinking that takes seriously the exposure, analysis, and transformation of societal and personal injustices and oppressions that affect those who usually matter least in society, as symbolized by poor Black women. *Womanist* theory is interdisciplinary and examines experience present in living, written, oral, visual, aural, sensual, and artistic texts to create its epistemology, hermeneutics, and philosophy. This involves ongoing intellectual, spiritual dialogue to prepare individuals to experience their own reality in a holistic manner. A *Womanist* liberative theory embraces engendering mutuality and community amid the responsibility and stewardship of freedom, and honors the *imago Dei*, the image of God, the essential goodness and divine beauty in all persons, and engages texts held as authoritative with a careful, critical, creative reading.

The body of knowledge and research of my own conceptualization of *Womanist* thought includes, but is not limited to, issues pertaining to the Bible and its narratives, theology, ethics, and contexts. Many seek to give the Bible religious and secular authority, both as a spiritual guidebook and as a political manual. They tend to confuse the actual texts of biblical narratives with oral myths about what is in the Bible, and disregard the literal words of the sacred text. Biblical scholarship often searches for a privileged reading toward some "Truth" about biblical history and ancient Israel; but some biblical stories, from the histories and allegories to the parables, contain multiple and often conflictual truths, have limited certainty, amidst irony and ambiguity, are often based on a psychological need of a reader, church, or other particular institution, to assert infallible credence to church authority and tradition. Some biblical scholarship attempts to reconstruct the sociopolitical and religious history of ancient Israel and the ancient Near East. The histories within the Bible relate to stories that are often reconstructed into particular contemporary ideologies, which are then used to justify the oppression of others. Other narratives, from music and art to literature and the living biotexts of individuals and communities, are also marvelous documents for reflecting on God and our covenantal life with God.

To unpack themes in general and violence in particular in texts, especially the Bible, one can explore and ask questions about what kinds of authority the texts have, who are the characters in them, by what rituals do they engage life, what are the dynamics around the use of language, and what are the various histories that are intersecting in a particular worldview. The questions surrounding theology that help us explore issues of violence include the complexities of the divinity, the nature of dialogue, and listening to God and our neighbors. The question of identity is essential for learning about the power and person of God and the ways in which the lives of human beings interact and affect community, particularly as they are intentional about an awareness of the very sacredness of life and of the world. This awareness of nature, of the sacred, enhances the capacity of one to experience hope and transformation toward engendering mutuality and community, while honoring the *imago Dei* in all persons. Living an embodied life, in touch with the personal and the communal, helps provide one with a foundation for a healthier, more holistic life. When divine and human relationships are central to one's well-being and when these relationships are grounded in faith, one can live a balanced ethical life.

Ethics is the discipline and experience of analyzing norms of human behavior towards assessing their lived and transformative values, and their subsequent related rules and codes of conduct.

With ethics emerges a concern for justice and for fostering the good for ourselves and our community so that we live a life of mutual respect where our daily goals help us assess what is important and we cherish those attributes that aid human flourishing. How we behave and conduct ourselves also relates to our emotional well-being and our own visibility. Visibility concerns who gets to speak versus who is never afforded the opportunity to speak for herself or himself. With ethics we also study individual and group integrity and how people live out their daily lives. Violence is unethical. Thus, when theologically assessing violence, it becomes even more important that we include all of the most difficult questions about what violence is and what happens in the wake of violent ways of being and acting.

One's sociohistorical context is critical to assessing violence, within all life, locating the roles and action of God and humankind. The context of the subject matter, the analyst, and the reader affects how the information is reported, interpreted, and understood. Within the context, we learn of people's stories or their autobiographies. Their autobiographies are the places from which we learn about their relationships with God, self, society, and violence in culture. *Culture* is the vital, engaged way of life shared by members of a society or communities and their capacity to catalog, organize, and communicate their experiences. *Community* pertains to a collective (or collectives) of persons with common, shared traits, interests, and rights and privileges in civil, political, and socioeconomic relationships; these collectives sometimes include racial and/or religious interests.

As a tool, Womanist theory can name, expose, question, and help transform oppression to champion the struggle for freedom for all people. Freedom is a gift and a right bequeathed by a personal God.

In sum, the landscape of violence is vast and far-reaching; it involves our personal and social, relational selves. Unnecessary violence is that which causes harm, destroys, maims, oppresses, manipulates, and discounts the *imago Dei* in other people. Theology, as God talk and language pertaining to how we relate to God and each other, is a lens that can help critique and ultimately transform violence. Theology does the analysis to name the wrong to heighten our awareness about violence and our complicity in it, and offers ways of being to help transform our own lives and others in society, through the grace of God. When analyzing violence, we can frequently identify a scapegoat. Scapegoat theory helps us understand how individuals and societies deal with violence by blaming someone who, due to status and social location, can be the recipient of the blame for the suffering and pain, often dissipating the escalating tension. We can see a scapegoat in many scenarios of violence. The forms of violence named earlier include: terrorism, natural disaster, racism, sexism, classism, war, and colonialism. All such violence involves destruction of the physical, mental, emotional, spiritual, financial, or sociocultural selves and community. An antithesis of violence is justice, where instead of doing harm, we opt for fairness, for equitable distribution, within right relationships. Womanist theological ethics is one lens that intentionally calls one to expose all oppression, to love all people, and to work to transform society in a way that lessens and transforms violence. Thinking theologically about violence can increase our awareness about what it is, how we can make a difference, and how we can live ethically and prevent our further complicity in societal violence.

> *Beautiful beings, made in God's image*
> *Thwarted, injured, through acts of violence*
> *By individuals, systems, institutions*
> *Scapegoats, taking the heat*
> *Dissipating tensions, masking realities;*
> *Violence, taking many forms*
> *Destruction globally*
> *Does not have to be*
> *When justice is a possibility.*

SKETCHES OF VIOLENCE IN THE BIBLE

INTRODUCTION

Reading and understanding the Bible is not easy. The language and sociohistorical, cultural settings are ancient. Yet, there is much that is relevant today. Playing detective, we will ask lots of questions of the text to help us see and hear what is on the surface and below. This chapter explores selected accounts of a variety of types of violence occurring in the Hebrew Bible and in the New Testament. Just as we cannot play soccer with tennis equipment or navigate a new location without a sense of direction and a map, we cannot begin to grasp violence in the Bible without asking a lot of questions. While many read the Bible for spiritual direction and personal devotion, to unearth the violence and know the impact of that violence requires a reading that can be uncomfortable for those seeking simple or easy answers. Reading from my Womanist biblical perspective presses me to ask questions about the violence amid oppressions stated in chapter 1; to be creative; to name the violence of humanity and that of God.

My lens for seeing uses suspicion with sensitivity to grasp what I read; to question the biblical text and its power for Christians; to appreciate the careful work on this text by biblical scholars; to honor its long history; and to acknowledge its misuse to justify bad causes. This is complex work, where some of my questions will be left unanswered. I can lend a creative ear to see how my life experience may contribute to the ways other interpretations and traditions have experienced the Bible. With courage, an analysis that allows comparisons provides a way to juxtapose various biblical stories to find common themes of violence, even if the texts and their themes seem antithetical. My reading of these texts embraces a commitment to hearing them in their ancient contexts. Doing so can afford discovering a just, appropriate living of these texts or ethics. Out of this commitment comes a candor that assures the naming of the oppression within the texts and questioning how we have used these texts amid faith. My curiosity supports searching these biblical texts to see how relationships between God and biblical characters unfold in a way that honors inclusivity, mercy, justice, and love. The seriousness of this work calls for a sense of the comedic that reminds us not to take ourselves so seriously that we fail to grow and to respect other ways of seeing; and, to be up-front about texts that I find jarring and unjust, knowing that others may disagree.

The selected Hebrew biblical texts are from Genesis, Exodus, and Judges. The Gospels serve as the texts for our New Testament excursion into violence. Most of the former have to do with types of family violence, the quest for liberation, leadership, land acquisition, and the issues around covenant, particularly the Abrahamic covenant of Genesis 12:1-3. The New Testament study explores the violence around the passion (life, suffering, death) of Jesus Christ. Violence moves throughout these texts, both divine and human. Much of the divine violence concerns curtailing the activities of human beings when they are disobedient. Much human violence involves disobedience to God and harm to others. Some of the human violence would not happen today in the same manner because of different sociocultural norms and more sophisticated technology (from weaponry to

satellites). This study calls into question divine and human violence, to show its commonness and its complexity. Some would
argue that divine violence is simply God's judgment and is always
justified. Some would argue that human violence is a product of
human nature as fallen or sinful creatures. My task is to prob-
lematize what we see and hear, how we interpret, and in some
instances to leave you with more questions than answers around
the notion of biblical violence.

As a child, I never thought of God as violent, though I knew
sometimes God gets angry. Sometimes God judges people when
they misbehave, but God might let them get away with doing
something bad and give them a second or third chance. God
might use a country or an individual to exact punishment on
God's chosen people, Israel and/or Judah. In "Sinners in the
Hands of an Angry God," a sermon by Jonathan Edwards
(1703–1758), who is widely acknowledged to be the most important and original philosophical theologian in the early United
States, Edwards hints that the biblical God is much more complex
than jolly old Santa Claus. In some Scriptures, it seemed like God
was testing people. Sometimes people tested God. Then I learned
that the Bible came out of an oral tradition; it took hundreds of
years for it to be recorded; and its original languages were Hebrew
and Aramaic for the Old Testament, and Greek for the New
Testament. I began to appreciate how incredible it is that the Bible
exists and that leaders of Judaism and Christianity sat in councils
to discern which books would be accepted in the canon. The
canon is the formal list of accepted books in the Bible.[1] If a person
committed some of the behaviors that God does in the Bible,
those acts would unequivocally be dubbed violent: they cause
harm, death, loss, and destruction. Of course, we cannot compare
God's acts with the acts of human beings, or can we? Since we
experience life as human beings, we use human or anthpomor-
phic language to talk about God: limited, biased language. Human
beings, known as scribes, heard and wrote down the Scriptures.

In the Bible, God is Creator and in charge. Ostensibly, God
gets to make decisions about what happens in the world. Is God
responsible, then, for everything people do? God has given us free

will, the capacity to make choices; thus much of what does happen on earth occurs because of direct human action. Sometimes when we experience God's violence in biblical texts, it seems that God's violent judgment is warranted; other times God's judgment seems too lenient, when particular characters find favor with God for no apparent reason even when they make big mistakes. Sometimes God's violence seems too harsh or unjust, when a biblical character's family ends up paying for what the ancestor did. When God's violence targets an individual, it may be beyond our capacity to understand. Such a scenario may also be the result of a human redactor or editor describing God's acts the way a human being might react. Generally, human violence in the Bible seems unwarranted and wrong, except when defending the life of another person. Just who is exacting the violence gets murky when God orders a group, say Israel, to engage in violence against another party to take the land (Gen 15:7-16), even when it involves them being taken into slavery, or when God uses another party to destroy Judah (2 Kgs 24:13-19; Jer 44:10-12). God also destroys others on behalf of Israel (Deut 32:42-44).

From a faith perspective, many acts of biblical, divine violence pertain to Israel being a chosen people in covenant with God in the Hebrew Bible. Covenants are about relationships. Several of the biblical covenants are contractual agreements of faith between God and Israel, where they will be God's people and God will be their God. God blesses Israel; Israel is to worship, praise, and obey God, and to live their lives based upon the laws of God. These Scriptures accept the underlying purpose of showing God as the one, only true God for an ancient people who had grown up in a society where most persons worshiped multiple gods, acknowledged by the commandment that says, "Thou shalt have no other gods before me." One way to read the Hebrew Bible is through the lens of God's covenantal promises to Abram in Genesis 12:1-3 to give him three things: land, a relationship with his people in perpetuity, and a son. (God changed Abram's name to Abraham in Genesis 17.)

Perhaps from God's viewpoint, divine violence is justified and serves a higher purpose of helping Israel to live an ethical life.

Some scenarios give us pause, however. The Canaanites, a people also created by God, were already living on the land that God promised to Israel. From a Canaanite vantage point, losing their land by command makes no sense. The Canaanites were minding their own business when they were summarily told to get off the land; and when they did not get off, fighting against them ensued at the behest of God. The text does not say that the Israelites tried to convert the Canaanites or that God wanted them to do so. The text does say that God told Israel to take the land that God had promised them. How would you feel if some evening, people knocked on your door and said you had to leave because God told them your property was theirs?

Conversely, in Isaiah 11:6, where wolf and lamb, leopard and goat, calf and lion lie down together, the message is one of peace and safety, a time of the messiah. Peace is not always easy to achieve. Sometimes it is complicated and paradoxical. Isaiah 53 states that the one who brings peace will also have to suffer. Isaiah 2:4 and Micah 4:3 speak of a time when weapons of war will be converted into implements for tilling the soil: instruments of death will become tools to support life. Here Isaiah and Micah support the notion of a divine prerogative for peace.

In the New Testament, within Christian covenantal life, God desires relationship with humanity and the church, as the body of Christ, where the church, the people who profess Christ as Lord, are to be an instrument of worship, nurture, instruction, and discipleship. In this relationship of love, reconciliation, and hope, God is Three in One: Creator, Son, and Holy Spirit. Some New Testament texts describe God's grace as mercy, an opportunity for hope and change, along with punishment for wrongdoing. Jesus often preaches the message of love and inclusion. When the rabbis ask him which of the 613 Jewish laws is the most important, he says to love God, yourself, and your neighbor (Matt 22:36-39). One could suggest that many acts of violence occur because love is absent. In his teachings, Jesus focuses on privileging the poor, a message of liberation for the oppressed. Often his teachings are antithetical to ancient cultural and religious practices.

VIOLENCE IN THE OLD TESTAMENT

Genesis

In the first creation account, Genesis 1:1–2:4, God takes seven days to make the world, out of chaos. Chaos involves violence as it pertains to a formless and disordered state of matter before creation of the cosmos; an instability, a shifting of power, of elements. God's birthing of the world occurred as light, sky, and land, followed by lights in the sky, creatures in the sky and water, and creatures on the land. The seventh day God rests. In Genesis 1:26-31, God said, Let us create humanity in our image, so that what begins in violence ends in an egalitarian relationship among a community of people who have dominion or stewardship, responsibility for the world, not permission for people to exploit the world's resources. In the second creation story (Gen 2:4-25), the order of creation and pantheon of characters shift. God creates earth, heavens, streams, and then the creature of the earth, whom God never names. Traditionally, people give the first human created the name Adam, from *adamah* (Hebrew for "earth").

God decides that this *adam* ought not be left alone, so God does another act of violence, taking one of Adam's ribs to construct Adam's helper. Then the violence of self-deception, disobedience, perhaps desperation unfolds. Having been told not to partake of the tree of the knowledge of good and evil (Gen 2:17), the couple disobeys, eats that fruit, deceiving themselves that they could become like God without consequence (Gen 3:2-6). Did the human couple think they could outwit or hide from the divine? Did they think about the consequences of their disobedience? Did they know who they were disobeying? Or, is this about divine ego that needs to sanction the disobedient couple? Why would God deny them access to this particular tree, since they had no previous role models or instruction? Perhaps the violence of the broken relationship involving a snake creates a kind of ménage à trois, between the earth creature, woman, and the serpent?

Some scholars suggest that the first creation story (Gen 1:1–2:4) is how God would see the beginnings of the world and humanity, and the second creation story (Gen 2:5ff) is from a human perspective. A careful reading of the second creation story in Genesis 2 and 3 shows that both Eve and the *adam* have choices. They both chose to eat the fruit. Eve did not have a primordial Uzi or AK-47 rifle forcing him to eat. (God never names Adam, while the male creature does name Eve.) The couple from the Garden did not fall out of anything; God expelled them. Perhaps the editors saw the expulsion as a necessary punishment to the human violence of self-deception and disobedience. Perhaps the editors envisioned that God's gift of creation has an implicit covenant; and because of the disobedience, God becomes more intentional about making explicit covenants with leaders of God's chosen people, as with Noah (Gen 9), Abraham (Gen 12, 17), and Moses (Exod 24).

Some persons justify patriarchy and sexual oppression of women via these two creation stories and use the New Testament for further justification. In reading Ephesians 5:22 as Scripture that commands wives to be subject, submissive, and inferior to their husbands, people often fail to read Scripture preceding immediately before that, which says believers are to be subject to one another out of reverence for Christ.

Several instances of violence occur between the dismissal of the first family and the divine/human covenant between Abram and God. The first murder occurs when Cain kills Abel, though one can question the notion of justice and violation of faith when God accepts Abel's offering of firstlings of his flock and disregards Cain's offering of grain, resulting in Cain's anger,[2] his feeling overwhelmed, and his murderous act. The violence in the Cain and Abel story is multifaceted: violence between brothers, violence between God and Cain.

In the Noah story (Gen 6–9), the texts recount rampant breaking of covenant, where the earth and all flesh are corrupt and filled with violence (Gen 6:11-12). Then God's violence causes massive destruction from the flood, which targets all of known creation. In the Tower of Babel story (Gen 11), community is dispersed and made to speak different languages. The text begins to focus more on family scenarios by introducing Abram and Sarai. There are hints of domestic violence, incest, and child abuse in the Abraham (Gen 16:3-6; 20:1-18, 22:1-14) and Lot (Gen 19:6-9, 30-38) sagas. Twice Abraham denies Sarah is his wife, once with Pharaoh and once with Abimelech, king of Gerar, exposing her to rape and molestation. Technically Abram does not lie, for Sarai is really Abram's half sister. The two sagas end differently. God visits Pharaoh's whole court with plagues for Pharaoh sleeping with Sarai. God comes to Abimelech in a dream, and God reopens the wombs of the women of Abimelech's house when he releases Sarai. The assault against Sarai—actually Abram, since Sarai is Abram's property—is viewed as an assault against God. Lot offers his two daughters as sexual hospitality to be gang raped and molested, whose "gift" is declined. Later, both daughters get him drunk, sleep with him, get pregnant, and give birth to ancestors of the Moabites and the Ammonites respectively.

Throughout the Hebrew Bible, assault against the community is assault against God; when assaults occur and children of Israel have remained faithful, God punishes those who do not follow the covenant. God also punishes Israel when they break the covenant. Whether a literary device or a recounting of history, Isaac follows his father and tells Rebecca to say she is his sister. This Philistine King Abimelech orders that no one harm them (Gen 20:1-14; 26:7-11). Rebecca also violates her maternal relationship and trust by robbing her son Esau of his blessing and conspires with her favorite son, Jacob, to lie to his father Isaac (Gen 27:4-36).

Abraham and Sarai are also complicit in domestic violence, as Sarai tells Abraham to take, or sleep with her servant Hagar, since Sarai is barren and cannot give Abraham an heir. Forced to sleep with Abram, Hagar conceives (Gen 16:1-4). Sarai gets upset with Hagar and sends her out to the desert. In the desert, Hagar is the only person to name God, *El Roi*, the God who sees (16:7-13). That same God sends her back into slavery, meaning Hagar was not her own person. Hagar is a forced surrogate mother, for her child is really to be Abram and Sarai's male heir.

Another victim of sexual assault is Dinah, daughter of Jacob and Leah. Shechem the Hivite seizes Dinah and rapes her (Gen 34); the text omits her mother, her father does nothing, but her brothers Levi and Simeon get angry. Shechem says he loves Dinah and is willing to pay the bride price. The brothers will agree to the marriage if all the male Hivites undergo painful surgery of circumcision. Afterwards, Levi and Simeon kill them all: deception produced mass genocide. Jacob's milquetoast response concerns his tribe, who now have difficulty from foreign persons, although not Dinah, for she is spoiled goods.

Along with murders, rape, and assault, the Joseph saga introduces jealousy and kidnapping (Gen 37:4, 11, 18-24). Upset about their father's favoritism, Joseph's brothers kidnap Joseph and sell him into slavery. Although Joseph rises to a position of authority in Potiphar's house, Potiphar's wife frames Joseph and lies, saying he raped her; but Joseph is vindicated. Joseph forgives his brothers and brings all of his family with him to Egypt.

The patriarchal and matriarchal stories of Genesis are full of dysfunctional families and varieties of violence. These stories parallel family matters today. Often within family, we know devastating, painful experiences of physical, emotional, and spiritual violence and abuse; matters that concern divine aegis. The God of Genesis creates us to be in relationship. Amid the beauty of creation, divine retribution and punishment happen to bring people back into right relationship, honoring their reality as human and God's reality as sovereign. Covenants between God and particular persons solidify the reconciliation, as if God admits the use of force and violence as necessary to get people's attention, and then wishes to reestablish the human ego and its freedom. The question remains, "Is God's use of violence always warranted?" Does the fact that God does the violence always make such violence acceptable?

Exodus

Exodus, the book many describe as a book of liberation, is liberation at a steep price for the Egyptians. Pharaoh decides he needs to control the Hebrew population, and they are in bondage to him. God sends Moses and Aaron to go and order Pharaoh to let God's people go (Exod 3:7–4:17). After Moses and Pharaoh meet and exchange words, Pharaoh hardens his heart. There is negotiation back and forth, and at points Pharaoh is willing to let them go. Yet God hardens Pharaoh's heart several times, meaning the Israelites will experience even more bondage. God sends nine plagues, which violate the environment and cause some deaths. When Pharaoh is about to bend, God hardens Pharaoh's heart after the ninth plague, then sends the death angel to kill the first-born males, human and animal, of *all* families in Egypt except those who paint their doorposts with blood. (Exod 11:4; 12:3-13). Did not this God create the Egyptians and the Israelites? Is the entire population of Egypt to blame for Pharaoh's mistakes? Is it really Pharaoh's fault if God intentionally hardens Pharaoh's heart so that God and only God gets the credit for liberating Israel? After Moses leads them out of Israel and they are near the Reed Sea, God hardens Pharaoh's heart again. All the Egyptian soldiers drown in pursuit.

Judges

After more than forty years in the desert, Israel continues its sojourn with violence—cyclical violence—in Judges. After Joshua dies, Israel's people violate the covenant by being unfaithful, and God responds. Though the book of Joshua puts a successful spin on Israel's conquest and settlement of Canaan, the Judges saga reflects a different viewpoint. Israel has not been so successful and their tolerance for the Canaanites is a theological faux pas. Since Israel did not follow God's command about getting rid of the Canaanites and their altars, God lets the Canaanites become Israel's adversaries and their gods overtake Israel (Judg 2:1-6), threatening Israel's own identity and relationship with God. As Israel's destiny unfolds through extended accounts and brief notices of judges who judge Israel or who deliver the people from oppression, a loosely recurring rhetorical deliverance formula of violence frames the storytelling: Israel does evil in God's sight; God gives Israel into oppression; Israel cries to God; God raises up a deliverer; the deliverer defeats the oppressor; the people are faithful while the deliverer is alive and the land rests, or is at peace; eventually the people continue their wrongdoing. Throughout the book, they worship alien gods and thus abandon God, who brought them out of Egypt. God gets angry and allows the Israelites to be plundered by their enemies, for God had warned them what would happen. One might argue for parental chastisement; either way, God allows violence against Israel. Since they are without leadership, God creates judges to deliver them from persecution, but Israel does not listen. When God raises up a judge, God is with the judge and the people obey. When a judge dies, Israel relapses and behaves worse than before. This cycle of violence repeats over and over, as Israel breaks covenant and worships other gods. Danna Fewell reminds us that this rhetorical deliverance formula has variations. By Jephthah's time, Israel's list of wrongs (apostasies) is considerably expanded (Judg 10:6); and when Israel cries out in repentance, Yahweh refuses to deliver them. There is no peace with the Jephthah or Samson story. Samson dies in captivity. The formula deteriorates and thus foreshadows Israel's future.[3]

Samson violates Yahweh's covenant. This dysfunctional judge's story reflects that forthcoming liberation comes despite Samson, not because of his merit. Israel's leadership sinks exponentially from the era of Moses to Samson. People decline, forgetting their covenant. They call to God only when they are in dire straits. Samson's story (Judg 13–16) begins with a promise of divine affirmation, as he is born a Nazirite: one separated or consecrated to God from birth to death (Judg 13:3-7). Samson becomes involved in conflict out of jealousy and vengeance, not theological conviction. His infatuation with Philistine women induces most of his violence. Known for his strength, Samson engages violence under God's will and spirit: he kills thirty men and takes their spoil (14:19), destroys fields of grain, olive groves, and vineyards using foxes (15:4-5); kills a thousand men with a donkey's jawbone (15:15). The same spirit that gives him his strength leaves him when his hair is shaved. Samson asks God for an act of revenge to pay back the Philistines for gouging out his eyes. God empowers Samson to pull down the house, and Samson asks to die with the Philistines. Samson kills more people with his temple destruction than he had killed during his lifetime (16:28-31).

The stories of Jephthah's daughter (Judg 11) and the secondary wife or concubine (Judg 19) are rife with violence against females. Jephthah, like Samson, seems an unlikely candidate for a judge. Son of a prostitute, his half brothers drive him away. Like David, this ancient "bad boy" gets involved with outlaws. When the Spirit of the Lord falls on him, Jephthah bargains with God. If God lets Jephthah overcome the Ammonites, he promises to offer whoever comes out of the doors of his house to meet him as a burnt offering. Who did Jephthah think would be coming out of his house? When he returns home, his daughter, his only child, runs out; and he tells her about his promise to God. His daughter seems content with the decision of her impending death, for she only asks to go off with friends for two months. She returns and Jephthah slaughters his own daughter as response to his promise. Since God told Abraham he would not need to sacrifice Isaac, as there is a ram in the bush, why do we not get similar language here? Are male progeny more valuable to God than daughters? Jephthah will murder his daughter as sacrifice to God in payment for the bargain that he made with God, but Abraham is restrained from sacrificing his son.

Not all women in Judges are victims; some have access to power. Judge Deborah, a prophetess, rallies Israel to fight against the Canaanites (Judg 4–5). Deborah works with Barak in the name of the Lord, God of Israel, to conquer Sisera, whom Deborah will deliver into Barak's hands. Barak is skittish and Deborah agrees to go with him, but tells him that God will allow a woman to capture Sisera. When defeat is imminent, Sisera flees and goes to Jael's tent; there had been good relations between Sisera's King Jabin and the clan of Jael's husband, the Kenites. Jael extends hospitality and assures him safety. After he goes inside and rests in her tent, she offers hospitality, then drives a tent peg into Sisera's temple (some scholars argue that it was his throat or ear), until it enters the ground; he dies. When Barak comes looking for Sisera, Jael shows him the dead man. Jael treacherously murders Sisera, after feigning hospitality, a gesture of utmost importance in the ancient Near East. Deborah had told us that God would allow this woman to overcome Sisera; thus a divinely sanctioned homicide. Deborah and Jael represent one of the combinations of two women who either kill or order murder in the Bible and the Apocrypha.[4]

Other than Deborah, no other judges presided over all Israel, nor were they jurists. Throughout the book of Judges, the rhetorical cycle of violence is a spiral that finds the nation of Israel in more trouble. Further removed from living their covenant with God, Israel declines; they engage in idolatry, wars, and elder abuse. There is no leadership, divine or human, and the community has disintegrated into chaos. The new rhetorical formula of violence notes that there is no king, and people do what they desire (Judg 17:6; 21:25; 18:1; 19:1).

The stories of creation; Abraham, Sarah, and Hagar; Noah; Joseph; the Exodus story of liberation; and the Judges cycle reflect some of the violence in the Hebrew Bible. The books telling the stories of the united and divided kingdoms of Israel and Judah and the protest of the prophets connected with their stories convey even more violence, including the battles pertaining to the fall of Jerusalem and Judah being captured by Babylon and the resulting exile.

Even the book of Psalms, the prayer book of the church, contains words of violence and vengeance. The God of the Old Testament is not only violent, however; this God is one of love and peace, one who desires relationships with people. This God wants to be worshiped and loves being loved. God offers the blessings of breast and womb (Gen 49:25), never forgets us (Isa 49:15), does not abandon or destroy, and offers mercy (Deut 4:31), offers comfort (Ps 23:4), and brings about restoration (Job 42:10). This God does violence and also ends it. Too often we tend to put God into a box of one-dimensional emotions and limited actions of extremes—God is either all love or all anger and judgment. Our study through the Old Testament shows that it is important not to stereotype this God as one who is angry and the New Testament God as one of love. The biblical stories of faith and history reflect a God who has a spectrum of emotions and a huge palette of feelings in response to human endeavor. In sum, sometimes God's violence seems harsh; sometimes it seems warranted; other times, it seems to bring about peace and reconciliation.

VIOLENCE IN THE NEW TESTAMENT: JESUS

In the vein of the Old Testament, the New Testament includes numerous stories of violence, particularly concerning the death of Jesus. Much remains unknown about his life, for the Gospels are focused on his teachings rather than on historical, chronological, or biographical data. The four New Testament Gospels represent four particular theological accounts by evangelists committed to inspiring faith in the risen Christ. The authors all wrote their testimonies decades after the death and resurrection of Jesus, and apparently subsequent to the Roman destruction of Jerusalem. The authors of the Gospels did not have direct knowledge of Jesus, but rather relied on oral traditions concerning Jesus' crucifixion handed down by those who had witnessed it. Philip A. Cunningham notes that the Gospels evolved over time, through three periods: (1) Jesus' ministry, including traditions about his actions and words from early in the first century; (2) apostolic, post-resurrection preaching about Jesus that emerged after his resurrection; and (3) the written Gospels, in which the authors collected, edited, and wrote down their accounts through their own interpretative lenses, insights, and experiences to serve their different audiences. Sometimes the Gospel authors take a defensive posture, other times they are responding to ongoing debates regarding the theological nature of Jesus as God and human. Not only were they working to make a case for Jesus as the Messiah and the new high priest, they were also living during an era when they were "going along to get along." That is, they were doing their best not to antagonize Roman authority in a world where religion, politics, and socio-economics were interrelated.[5] That each evangelist had a particular agenda in writing a particular Gospel is critical, particularly when the substance of faith is often the subject of contemporary media expressions.

Contrary to popular belief, Mel Gibson's *The Passion of the Christ* is not a historical account of the death of Jesus based on the Gospels or medical, forensic evidence. *The Passion* is overwhelmingly based on the anti-Semitic writings of an eighteenth-century mystic, Anne Catherine Emmerich.[6] In Gibson's rendering, the film is a "Braveheart type" victim-hero saga, rife with unrelenting violence, in which a faction of Jews led by Caiaphas, the high priest, coerce a pitiful Pilate into giving Jesus the death penalty.[7] Contrary to Emmerich/Gibson, a study of the four Gospels *does not* reveal or corroborate a merciless, brutal beating of Jesus by priests or a crowd.[8] Modern playwrights, cinematographers, and any others creating depictions of Jesus' passion must be vigilantly aware of the tensions and differences within and between the Gospels, the polemical and apologetical texts that were derived decades after the actual events, and avoid synthesizing the four divergent accounts into a single Fifth Gospel. Mark's Jesus is alone, and only the centurion, of all the followers and detractors, knows who Jesus is. The Lukan Jesus is focused on healing, wellness, and reconciliation. The Matthean Jesus focuses on replicating Israel's salvation history. The Johannine Jesus is clearly divine and always in charge.[9] Codifying the thinking of most scholars today, Vatican II noted that "neither all Jews indiscriminately at that time nor Jews today can be charged with the crimes committed during [Jesus'] passion . . . all must take care, lest . . . they teach anything which is not in accord with the truth of the gospel message or the spirit of Christ."[10] Bearing this in mind, we turn to glimpse some of the details of Jesus' life and death.

According to Matthew, the aftermath of Jesus' birth unfolds amid violence. After the wise men visit the family, Joseph takes Mary and the infant Jesus and they flee to Egypt after being warned in a dream: Herod is searching for the child to destroy him. Furious at being tricked by the wise men, Herod orders all the children in and around Bethlehem who are two years old or under to be murdered (Matt 2:9-16). In this story, Matthew wants his readers to recall the story of Moses, who escaped the pharaoh's command that Hebrew boys be killed (Exod 1–2) and delivered his people from bondage. For Matthew, Jesus is a "new Moses."

The Gospel writers also tell the story of Jesus' death in ways that express their understanding of who Jesus was. In the Gospel of Mark, for example, Jesus' passion involves betrayal, dishonesty, taunting, collusion, and physical brutality. In chapter 14, Judas secretly betrays Jesus to "the chief priests"; Jesus later predicts that "the Son of Man" will be betrayed while eating the Passover meal with the disciples. He also predicts that all the disciples will desert him, and they all deny any complicity. Jesus goes with the disciples to pray in the garden of Gethsemane, and they cannot stay awake; thus Jesus experiences betrayal, forsakenness, and loneliness—his disciples violate the trust to keep watch. Judas betrays Jesus with a kiss, and "a crowd with swords and clubs, from the chief priests, the scribes, and the elders" comes to arrest Jesus. The disciples scatter.

Mark then describes a meeting in which Jesus is questioned by the high priest, who asks him whether he is the Messiah. Jesus answers in the affirmative and again refers to himself as "the Son of Man." Jesus is condemned for this blasphemous statement, and some there spit on and strike him. He experiences cruelty: disrespect and humiliation with the pain. He is bound over "as a self-appointed king who would undermine Roman authority"[11] to Pilate, the Roman governor, who asks Jesus whether he is the "king of the Jews." A "crowd"[12] asks Pilate to release the rebel[13] Barabbas[14] and crucify Jesus. Pilate has Jesus flogged, a standard Roman practice before crucifixion to hasten death, then Roman soldiers put a purple robe (representing royalty) and a crown of thorns on Jesus and mock him as "king of the Jews." (Contrary to Mark's account, no historical evidence exists to substantiate that Pilate was under the thumb of any crowds or Judean leadership.)[15] Then they take Jesus to a designated place and crucify him.

Crucifixion was an ancient Roman death penalty for insurrection. Crucifixion, especially used among the Persians, Carthaginians, Romans, and Egyptians, meant a painful death by slow asphyxiation. A typical Roman flogging was done with a whip with pieces of bone or metal tied into its thongs; the pain and blood loss from the flogging would have left Jesus in a weakened condition for his crucifixion. He may have also experienced bloody sweat or hematidrosis, which can happen when a person has experienced intense emotional stress. Crucifixion was a humiliating punishment "reserved only for slaves, foreigners, revolutionaries, and the vilest of criminals."[16] The condemned man was often forced to carry the crossbar to the crucifixion site. There, the Romans would usually nail the victim through his wrists and feet, rather than tie the wrists to the crossbar, and then the crossbar and man were lifted onto the upright post, to which his feet would be nailed or tied. A sign with the charge against the man was placed above his head. The length of time one could survive crucifixion likely depended on the severity of the flogging. Hanging on a cross also meant that one could not breathe normally, and so death would result from a combination of shock, exhaustion, and lack of oxygen. Death could be assured by breaking the legs; and the Romans often stabbed the victim with a sword or spear before releasing the body. Though scientists remain uncertain as to whether Jesus' exact cause of death was cardiorespiratory failure or cardiac rupture, medical and historical evidence indicates that he died before being stabbed in his side.[17]

Betrayed and abandoned, Jesus experiences a horrific, violent death. While fearful, cowardly male disciples were long gone, several women followers from Jesus' ministries in Galilee and Jerusalem watch from near by: Mary Magdalene, Mary the mother of James the younger and of Joses, and Salome. On the day of resurrection, Easter, women are present for Jesus' post-resurrection experience. In all four Gospels, Mary Magdalene is the apostle to the apostles, the one Jesus admonishes and invites to go and tell the good news, to spread the gospel: to proclaim that Jesus lives. Contrary to tradition and popular culture, Mary Magdalene was not a prostitute. She was a follower of Jesus.

41

What did Mark want his first readers to understand about Jesus from his account of Jesus' crucifixion and death? One clue is the repetition of the phrase "Son of Man" in Mark 14–15. In Daniel 7:13-14, "one like a son of man" appears in the presence of "the Ancient One" and is given dominion over all peoples and nations. In Mark, Jesus probably means to identify himself with this exalted figure, but he offers a surprising twist: the Son of Man will have to suffer.[18] Jesus is thus a model for Mark's non-Jewish readers who may also have experienced persecution.

Unfortunately, over time texts about Jesus' crucifixion have been used to justify violence against Jews. The Gospels were written decades after the time of Jesus. As the gospel spread outward from Jerusalem, more and more Gentiles converted to Christianity. Occasionally there were conflicts between synagogues and churches, which made it easier for the converted Gentiles to see themselves as experiencing mistreatment in the synagogues by the Jewish leaders, just as Mark said Jesus did. Texts such as Mark 14–15, which repeatedly mention "the chief priests, scribes, and elders," provided support for those determined to see Jews as responsible for Jesus' death—which in turn seemed to justify violence against Jews generally, as Christ-killers.[19]

We must not make the same mistake. The Gospel writers arranged the traditions they had about Jesus in particular ways in order to make a theological polemic about who they perceived Jesus to be. Matthew, Mark, Luke, and John were not newspaper reporters, giving detailed accounts of what they themselves had witnessed. They wrote their accounts decades after the fact. They did not go to libraries and research the passion events. Nevertheless, they also do not simply say, "Here's who I think Jesus was." Instead, their theology, their testimony of faith, comes through in the way they tell their stories about Jesus: "This is what we say Jesus wanted all to believe."

A full appreciation of the events narrated by the Gospels will also take into account the sociocultural context in which Jesus and his early followers lived. Palestine was under Roman occupation. The "Pax Romana" (Roman peace) was kept through brutal oppression. Rome and its representatives, including Pilate, allowed no rebellion and quickly and violently put down any sign of dissent. Pilate was eventually removed from his post because of his extreme brutality toward the Jewish population. In Mark, Jesus is ultimately crucified for accepting the title "king of the Jews." From Rome's perspective, there could be only one ruling power in Palestine.

Further, Jews in Jesus' day did not all respond to life under Roman occupation in the same way. Some cooperated with Roman administration in an attempt to keep the peace. Most wanted to see Rome driven out of the land, and resented their religious leadership for collaborating with Rome. Some of them resorted to violent resistance. Most tried to maintain as normal a life as possible. Therefore, when we read in Mark that Jesus is brought before the high priest, chief priest, scribes, and elders, we must not think that they represented the majority of Jews or that Caiaphas and his brethren had any real authority. In the end, the number of Jews involved in Jesus' crucifixion and death was minuscule. Jesus was crucified because Roman authorities perceived him as a terrorist and a threat and wanted to keep others from stirring up the people against them.[20]

What does Jesus say about violence? Some see Matthew 10:34, where Jesus comes to bring a sword not peace, as affirmation of aggression and violence. Many scholars suggest this is a misinterpretation. Rather, Jesus warns that persecution will come to Christians, and that ultimately truth will divide the world for we have different interpretations and understandings about God, life, faith, and truth. Words that seem to endorse violence are those that intimate that followers of Jesus must be willing to give up everything; they may face persecution. In the Temple with the money changers (Matt 21:12ff; Mark 11:15ff; Luke 19:45; John 2:13ff), Jesus causes no harm. He tells them to get out and not desecrate the Temple: a "dramatic disruption." In ancient culture, his wisdom language was not considered violent. Some of our staunchest enemies are those from our own households (Matt 10:36). In sum, there are times when God orchestrates violence for the greater good of God's chosen people; other times divine violence seems too harsh. Biblical violence is complex and needs to be heard and reckoned with, story by story, for a better grasp of Scripture.

What have we learned? Violence exists in the Bible through divine and human activity. Though some violence may seem uncalled for, or unjustly pronounced on people by God, divine violence usually occurs to curb human disobedience. Human violence involves acts of disobedience, a need to control, and self-aggrandizement. Theologically, the Bible sees divine violence as warranted and most human violence as disobedience, or sin. A Bible reader can know that violence exists and is not always understandable. Yet, it is important not to deny the violence or forget that the biblical sociohistorical, cultural context is different from our reality. From a Womanist ethical perspective, we must name violence, even when it is uncomfortable, and note who does violence, the results, and how the text understands what transpired. A Womanist reading views with suspicion unnecessary violence that causes oppressions of racism, classism, sexism, or violence that produces any harm and wonders about the Bible's purpose, who shaped the divine and human characters, and what we might learn not to do from biblical insights. Often, scapegoats appear where one person or a group of persons gets blamed or are used to resolve a crisis: e.g., Jephthah's daughter pays with her life for her dad's impetuousness; those without blood on doorposts pay for Pharaoh's wrongs. Biblical violence reminds us that human beings are capable of doing bad things, with and without cause. Revealing these acts of violence gives us an opportunity to learn how people do violence and, therefore to do what we can to avoid engaging in violence ourselves.

> *Revelation about God*
> *About humanity*
> *We come to know*
> *The Bible tells us so;*
> *Much of the good*
> *Some of the bad*
> *The violence here below.*

SKETCHES OF VIOLENCE IN CULTURAL NARRATIVES

FROM CLASSIC LITERATURE TO GRIMM'S FAIRY TALES

Much of the required reading in a classical education is rife with violence, including the English bard's plays and the Greek tragedies. In this chapter we review a Shakespearean play, *Othello*; Toni Morrison's novel *The Bluest Eye*; the television series *CSI: Crime Scene Investigation*; a film, *The Silence of the Lambs*; a Grimm's fairy tale, *Hansel and Gretel*; and a video game, *Grand Theft Auto*, to glimpse the proliferation of violence and the underlying theological issues in classic literature and popular media, in historical and contemporary settings: (1) What do characters' behavior traits reveal about their temperament, self-esteem, and control issues that violate others? (2) Does the story involve abuse of power? (3) How does the scapegoat mechanism function? (4) How does oppression indicate violence? (5) How does theological reflection increase our awareness about violence, and about how we can live ethically and prevent our own further personal complicity? Using these questions to analyze narratives helps us reflect on the ubiquity of violence and the presence of theology in culture, and helps us discern ways we can avoid our own daily complicity in violence.

OTHELLO

William Shakespeare's plays are rendered globally on the stage and adapted for cinema and opera. *Othello*,[1] a tragedy of embittered love, involves a cataclysmic triangle: Othello, Desdemona, and Iago. *Othello*, at its basic level a domestic tragedy, involves interpersonal and personal violence: deception, bigotry, envy, treachery, struggle, passion, and crime. With the emotional, destructive behaviors common to domestic abuse, this play provides insight into love triangles, outcomes of coercion, manipulation, and objectification of humanity. In toto, *Othello* involves race, class, and gender violence. Othello is a Moor, considered swarthy during Elizabethan times, usually portrayed as a black man. Other major characters are Venetian, Italian. Iago manipulates Bianca, viewed as Cassio's lowerclass mistress. All the women end up being abused or used.

Iago, Othello's soldier, spies on Othello, a Moor, for Roderigo because Roderigo wants Desdemona. Manipulative Iago hates Othello; infuriates Brabantio, Desdemona's father; and tells Othello that Roderigo turned Brabantio against Othello. Lies beget violence and lead toward crises: Othello and Roderigo both desire Desdemona. Iago and Cassio both want to be Othello's assistant. Surreptitiously, Iago scapegoats Othello. Othello and Desdemona marry. Brabantio believes Othello has wronged Desdemona, but Othello gets called away.

While Brabantio complains about Othello, Othello recounts their love story, which Desdemona confirms. The Duke tells Brabantio to accept the marriage and orders Othello to Cypress. Desdemona will follow with Iago. Iago promises Roderigo that Desdemona will tire of Othello. To undermine Othello, Iago uses Roderigo and lies saying that Cassio and Desdemona are lovers.

Weeks later, Desdemona arrives with Iago, who realizes that Cassio may love Desdemona. Iago lies, telling Roderigo that Desdemona could still be his. After Othello arrives, Iago claims Desdemona and Cassio are lovers. Iago plies Cassio with alcohol and then tells Montano, former governor, that Cassio is alcoholic. At Iago's bidding, Roderigo attacks Cassio; Cassio wounds Roderigo and Montano. Othello demotes Cassio. Iago comforts Cassio and advises him to ask Desdemona to be his advocate with Othello. Iago tells his wife, Emilia, to make sure Desdemona and Cassio talk so Othello can see them together.

Emilia tells Cassio that Othello wants him as his lieutenant again. Desdemona promises Cassio that Othello still loves him, and she will intervene. Iago convinces Othello to doubt Desdemona's devotion. After Desdemona drops a handkerchief Othello had given her, Emilia gives it to Iago. Iago places the handkerchief near Cassio's home; unknowingly he finds and claims it. Iago tells an enraged Othello he saw Cassio with Desdemona's handkerchief. Persuaded, Othello curses Desdemona and orders Iago to kill Cassio. Othello will handle Desdemona.

Desdemona frets, knowing the missing handkerchief will upset Othello. Othello inquires and Desdemona promises it will be found. Desdemona tells Cassio her efforts to help are failing. Cassio gives Othello's handkerchief to Bianca, Cassio's mistress, who starts to copy its patterning. Iago fuels Othello's distrust by claiming Cassio said he had slept with Desdemona. When Iago meets with Cassio, Iago talks about Bianca, further angering a hidden Othello, who thinks their focus is Desdemona. Bianca gives Cassio the handkerchief. Taunted by Iago, Othello decides to strangle Desdemona in her bed. Iago vows to kill Cassio. Othello returns home, and Desdemona wonders why she has so offended her beloved Othello. Othello questions Emilia about Desdemona's unfaithfulness, disregards her comments of innocence, and tells Desdemona the problem is her infidelity. In conversation, Desdemona and Emilia try to understand Othello's strange behavior.

Iago and Roderigo wait to ambush Cassio. Roderigo assaults Cassio; Cassio wounds Roderigo. Iago wounds Cassio. Iago stabs Roderigo. Othello enters Desdemona's bedroom, convinced killing her is for her own good. He kisses his sleeping wife, and Desdemona awakens. Despite her pleas, Othello smothers Desdemona.

Othello lets Emilia enter. She says Iago killed Roderigo. Othello confesses, and Emilia tells the truth about the handkerchief; Iago stabs her and escapes. Emilia criticizes Othello for killing Desdemona. Lodovico, Montano, Cassio, and the now-prisoner Iago enter. Othello stabs Iago, and claims killing Desdemona was honorable. The murders instigated by Iago are revealed. Iago confirms the lie about Desdemona. Realizing he had been duped, Othello commits suicide. The drama ends with four violent deaths: three murders and a suicide. The one who cuckolded and manipulated everyone shuffles off in chains.

Tragically, *Othello* exposes an anguished outcome when a masterful manipulator plays others' weaknesses. Iago abused people. He turned husband against wife and friend against friend. The duplicity, deceit, three murders, and a suicide press the theological question of human nature or Christian anthropology. Christians assume people, made in God's image, are to love, and can make choices. *Othello* signals the cost of those choices, human fragility and vulnerability; and how duress triggers violence. When evidence shows Othello's impaired reasoning, Desdemona stays, typical of denial amid domestic violence. Iago's behavior reflects hatred and abuse of power. Theologically, people need to handle power responsibly and need to exercise freedom with responsibility and integrity. To assure such integrity requires communal accountability and support. Communities and nation-states need to value and respect human life and embrace ethics based upon healthy societal and personal values.

To avoid scapegoating requires naming oppressions, developing new social paradigms of relating to people who are different, and working to transform negative systemic behavior. What Othello most desired he loses by his own hand. Iago destroys everyone else. Othello's destruction in his public and private worlds mirrors the life of a little Black girl who self-destructs in another way in a Nobel Prize–winning novel.

THE BLUEST EYE

Toni Morrison's *The Bluest Eye*[2] is a heartrending, illuminating novel about tensions and contradictions via societal racial, sexual, and class violence and conflicts about the marginalized. Morrison's story begins with the conclusion: one fall, marigolds that the MacTeer sisters planted did not grow in an oppressed Black community in Lorraine, Ohio. The protagonist, Pecola Breedlove, lives with the MacTeers because her dad, Cholly Breedlove, burned down the family's apartment. Pecola's mother, Mrs. Breedlove, stays with her employers. Pecola's brother, Sammy Breedlove, stays with relatives. The Breedloves' tragic, degrading situation involves societal and self-inflicted violence. They project ugliness; everyone perceives them as ugly, a catalyst for domestic violence. Pecola's insecurity ensues from her parent's pathologies and a violent society. Mrs. Breedlove escapes by going to movies, adopts the beauty projected as whiteness, and abandons her family.

Abandoned by his father before birth and his mother after, his Aunt Jimmy raised Cholly Breedlove. After her funeral when Cholly was fourteen, he was forced by white hunters to have sex with a girl cousin. Cholly scapegoated the girl. Abandoned by his father a second time, Cholly abandons all emotional ties. Drunk, Cholly rapes eleven-year-old Pecola. Desperate for blue eyes, the marker of beauty, Pecola seeks help from Soaphead Church, alleged spiritualist, charlatan, and pedophile. Convinced by Church that she now has blue eyes, a pregnant Pecola plummets into self-delusion and deception. The adults say it would be best if Pecola's child dies. Claudia and Frieda pray hoping the child will live, but Pecola's child dies, and she goes mad. Her imaginary friend asks her about the rape, her mother's abuse, and the second rape by her dad. Pecola repeatedly asks, "Are my eyes *the bluest eyes?*" No one could love her enough. Coming full circle, Claudia, one of the MacTeer sisters, recalls when the marigold seeds did not grow.

Pecola knows that she has no worth, no value, and is not lovable. All adults, black and white, seem to love only white blue-eyed children. Pecola's idolatrous worship of Shirley Temple, the idol for blonde hair and blue eyes, brings tragedy. With naive devotion, Pecola yearns for blue eyes, to obtain her parents' affection.[3] Both mother and daughter embody the ugliness of victimized sexism, racism, and classism, inflated and internalized. When Pecola takes action toward her transformation, she goes to a "Reader, Adviser, and Interpreter of Dreams," an insipid, ego-centered, obsessive-compulsive con man.[4]

Soaphead Church, "whose business is dread,"[5] desires things, despises people. He fixates on children's bodies. He really wants to grant Pecola's wish to have blue eyes. Little pregnant Pecola leaves believing her eyes are now blue.[6] Soaphead Church blames God for all of the pain and wrongs of the world: "Evil existed because God had created it. . . . God had done a poor job, and Soaphead suspected that he himself could have done better."[7]

In Morrison's macroscopic imagination, we experience difference, dissonance, tragedy, poverty, racism, sexism, misogyny, and patriarchy, framed by chapter headings with themes from a Euro-American, middle-class Dick and Jane primary school reader, celebrating dominant cultural norms. Dick and Jane signify white privilege, systemic violence, and the demonization of Blackness. The Breedloves are scapegoats, the demonized other. They desire acceptance, love, and freedom, but the family collapses into ontological, incarnated ugliness. Ugliness personifies the pain and violence born of deceit, hatred, crippling codependency, self-loathing, projection, and self-annihilation. Ugliness and hatred—patriarchy, misogyny, white privilege, ridicule, poverty, intraracial racism, and external racism—snares, defiles, and kills Pecola, spiritually and psychologically.

Pecola's neurotic, misguided quest for "shared, ordinary, mutual engagement, results from her distorted cosmology as a pubescent African-American female in the United States."[8] Her orchestrated world evokes a symphony of blue-eyed blondness. Pecola's countering solo is a wailing futile dissonance, a cacophonous dirge symbolizing her dysfunctional family and a world that denies her agency, voice, meaning, health, love, understanding, and security. Pecola's mother visualizes her *in utero* child to fit her fantasy of white cinematographic beauty. Cholly "loves" Pecola enough to violate, rape, and impregnate her. The Blackness and poverty surrounding the Breedlove family is pervasive, but their ugliness is unique: "anonymous misery."[9] Their ugliness concretizes their victimhood: "No one could have convinced them that they were not relentlessly and aggressively ugly. . . [You] wondered why they were so ugly. . . . Then you realized that it came from conviction, their conviction."[10]

Mr. Breedlove wears ugliness as maniacal martyrdom, speaking death to his family's hopes and dreams.[11] Son Sammy uses ugliness as self-destructive empowerment. Pecola's ugliness shields her from others.[12] Mrs. Breedlove's delusions make her beat Pecola. Mr. Breedlove rapes his daughter. Pecola's insecurity and Sammy's destructive behavior numb them and escalate their violence and rage. Pecola's parents' pathologies destroy them and their reality, and they taunt each other toward enraged depravity.[13] Their sick, mimetic desire for the unattainable and their pathological self-hate allow blonde, blue-eyed ideologies to destroy mutuality and social progress.[14] Pecola is everyone's scapegoat. No one could love Pecola; she has no place in the idealistic *Dick and Jane* primer which disavowed lived racial diversity. Pecola is powerless; she has no ability to name, define, and perceive reality.[15]

The ugliness that is personified in *The Bluest Eye* is misbegotten anguish.[16] The spiritual, physical, psychological, and philosophical lynchings of one's gender, racial/ethnicity, and class group by another are misbegotten anguish. Such evil exists globally. As Pecola's life spirals to insanity, we see the levels of pathology created by multiple oppressions. Pecola cannot and will not know love and affirmation. The MacTeer sisters understand that no one could love Pecola enough. Most people know and experience God because others model the love of God for them. But Pecola has never experienced love, though once she did know some kindness. Pecola is cursed and abandoned even *in utero*, because Mrs. Breedlove fantasizes about a white child she can never have. When mammals do not bond with their mother, they do not thrive. Theologically, to be abandoned, disrespected, abused, and misused is antithetical to knowing God and being in a healthy relationship. Pecola is doomed, for those around her cannot create community with her, so she cannot experience communion by connecting with power that brings about equity and healing. The complex ugliness born of systemic, multiple oppressions produces ridicule, objectification, violence, and callous disregard, a person rife with ignorance, fear, naiveté, and devoid of hope.

CSI

Just as classic and popular works of fiction teach us about humanity, life, and God, popular television dramas, like *CSI: Crime Scene Investigation*, show how art often imitates life, as life often imitates art. This primetime popular television sensation is the impetus for academic forensic science courses and programs throughout the United States. Created by Anthony Zuiker, this CBS crime series is set in Las Vegas, Nevada. The viewer observes crime scene analysis and results of murderous violence through the city's Crime Scene Investigations work. The multicultural, intergenerational team has male and female leadership. The audience learns little about their personal lives. The focus is on dissecting the crime: what violence occurred, how it happened, who did it, how they did it, where they are now, and how they shall be apprehended, not the adjudicatory conclusion. Criminologists use technological, state-of-the-art forensic equipment and analytical procedures to solve crimes that seem unsolvable. One cannot help questioning the nature of human life: What does it mean to be made in the image of God? How does one determine the value of an individual life; and how ought one to treat the body of a human being in death? In death, is the body absent the mind and the spirit or soul, and do those absences mean we can do anything we desire to the body?

Crime scene investigation involves forensic scientists, medical examiners who use observation, experimentation, and theory to analyze biological, chemical, or physical samples taken into evidence, to provide the proof police need to bring the case to court. A medical examiner, usually an appointed government official (often a medical doctor), has medical training to perform an autopsy on bodies with traumatic, suspicious, or uncertain cause of death. The medical examiner or coroner investigates a death, notably when death is unnatural, mysterious, or sudden. Some forensic specialists[17] are forensic anthropologists who study the remains. Their skills are needed when bodies have decomposed, are decapitated, or have been destroyed in some manner. They listen to the dead to support finding and identifying bodies and body parts, then determine the cause and time of death.

The *CSI* criminologists work in teams of subspecialists to investigate the inexplicable cases. Each week they have two cases to solve. Fluid camerawork, quick tableaus or mosaics, juxtaposed images, and surrealistic scene transitions tell the story over subtle background music, which can dull the audience's sensitivity to the cutting and "violation of the body" that occurs. Detailed autopsies and testing evoke a violation. The deceased often merely becomes a series of test results, dissected parts, and DNA stains. The modes, magnitude, and means of death are complex and varied. Most of the deaths are murders.

The murders include poisonings, hangings, gunshots, asphyxiations, hit and run, blunt force trauma, stabbings, and drownings. Rarely are the deaths self-inflicted or natural. Once the crime is reported, the criminologists process the scene. They secure the crime scene, dust for fingerprints, check for blood spatters, fibers, hairs, tissue, trajectory of bullets, footprints, and tire treads. They check for weapons, signs of forced entry, and determine an approximate time of death. The coroners bag the victim's hands to protect evidence and place the body in a body bag to remove it for autopsy. The medical examiner checks the body for marks, cuts, surface wounds, contusions, and possible leads to the cause of death. The autopsy involves a surgical procedure on the deceased to examine body tissues, internal organs, and body fluids. As the coroner follows with the autopsy, criminologists search the crime scene for evidence. The autopsy is crucial in bringing the criminal to justice, but too invasive for some persons and groups. Some cultures and religions find removing any body part before burial abhorrent, prohibiting autopsy. Other traditions forbid autopsy except when physicians believe the results will help medical science preserve human life. When families prohibit autopsy, the criminologists are as sensitive as they can be and use external means such as CT scans and MRIs to support their investigation.

The autopsy report and crime scene reveal the habits, desires, sensibilities, and relationships of the crime victim. By exploring their relationships, lifestyle, and priorities, the criminologists often discern potential suspects. On *CSI*, unlike real life itself, the investigators use state-of-the-art forensic technology to solve a seemingly unsolvable crime in forty minutes. No crime is unsolvable. Technology; investigative, human ingenuity; and the perpetrator's human callousness provide the clues toward solving the crime.

What do we learn theologically about ourselves and life through this dramatic series? We human beings have created copious ways to destroy each other, showing a distinct disregard for human life. The notion of humanity created in God's image becomes irrelevant. We objectify someone to kill him or her. Such disregard devalues life, community, ethics, and healthy spirituality. The investigation shows the creative, inventive, problem-solving, and compassionate gifts of the human mind, in despicable situations. For society to grasp and live out what it means to be made in the image of God requires justice for all. We cannot allow privilege, power, prestige, or property to trump justice. Theologically, violence between humans as on *CSI*, other than for defense, is wrong. Every person is to be accorded respect. Respect is one aspect of love. This love involves *filia*, the love of brother and sister; *eros*, sexual love; and *agape*, love that gives unconditionally, without expecting anything in return. As our physical bodies are temples, all persons' minds, bodies, and spirits need to be accorded respect. To do less is unconscionable, is offensive to God, and erodes the human spirit and the potential to become more like God.

HANSEL AND GRETEL

The story of *Hansel and Gretel*,[18] a Grimm Brothers' folktale, involves multiple violences: betrayal, abandonment, murder, and cannibalism. A poor woodcutter, his wife, and two children, Hansel and Gretel, fall on hard times. The woodcutter cannot make enough to feed them. Theologically, the family's financial status echoes gross global poverty, which presses the stewardship question and responsible use of our resources. The next theological issue concerns how we deal with stereotypes and the reality that not all human beings choose to live righteous lives. How do we detach from hurtful people with love, not become victims or hate them?

The father is anxious because they only have enough bread for the two adults. His wife says they should leave the children in the forest; wild animals would devour them, otherwise all four will die. The children overhear the conversation. Hansel goes outside and fills his coat pockets with white pebbles so they can trace their way back home. When they are deep in the forest, the father tells the children to build a fire. Hansel and Gretel gather brushwood and light a fire, and their stepmother tells them to lie down and rest; the parents will return.

Hansel and Gretel sit by the fire hearing the supposed sound of their father's wood-axe. The sound is a branch he rigged to blow back and forward. The parents violate parental trust and abandon the children. When they finally wake up, Hansel comforts Gretel and promises they will find the way home. Under the full moon, they follow the shiny pebbles and return home. The stepmother blames the children for being so late. Their father is thrilled, for he had dreaded abandoning the children.

Again the family falls on hard times and the stepmother's option is to get rid of the children. The father says no, but the stepmother says he must cooperate. Again the children overhear them. The stepmother takes the children deeper into the forest, and they fall asleep. This time, there are no pebbles or crumbs. Later, walking deeper into the forest, they come upon a bird that leads them to a house of bread and cakes. They hear: "Who is nibbling at my house?" An old woman feeds the children and promises them no harm. She is a "wicked witch" with poor vision. She entraps, fattens, cooks, and eats children: a trickster and a cannibal. The witch locks up Hansel. She makes Gretel cook and feed Hansel so he will get fat. Since the old woman cannot see, Hansel extends a little bone to her so she thinks he is not gaining weight: a survivor, not a victim. After four weeks, the witch is ready to eat him. Gretel implores God to help them, as Hansel had before. The witch tells Gretel that nothing and no one can help them.

The old woman pushes Gretel to the oven. Aware of her deceitfulness, Gretel says she does not know how to work the oven. As the old woman shows Gretel, Gretel pushes the old woman into the oven and shuts and locks the iron door. The witch burns to death. Gretel frees Hansel, they rejoice, run from the witch's forest, and return home. Their father is overjoyed. Their stepmother is dead. Gretel and Hansel give their treasures to their dad, all anxiety ends, and they live together in perfect happiness.

Fairy tales engage themes from fantasy, magic, joy, and escape to recovery, grief, loss, harm, and consolation amid violence that manifests itself as vicious brutality, egregious cruelty, merciless aggression, excessive carnage, and deadly hostility.[19] Fairy tales are rife with imagery of dead animals, bloodstained tools, burning witches, and poisoned protagonists. Globally, fairy tales seem to invoke the supernatural, exotic, and poetic with the violent. Fairy tales, part of adult cultural oral storytelling traditions dating back long before literacy, became the norm to pass the time or share traditions, for children's story hours and bedtime rituals. Based on volumes sold, fairy tales come in third, surpassed only by the Bible and Shakespeare. Though the Grimm brothers tempered their bawdy humor because people read their stories to children, interestingly, children usually experience cathartic pleasure listening to stories of physical or burlesque violence.[20]

What does the level of violence in children's stories say about society? These levels show we glorify violence and get an adrenaline rush from confrontation and bloodletting. Heightening our awareness to violence requires we become more mindful. We must unmask and name prejudices and stereotypes to examine the little truth and larger lies behind stereotypes and to learn about those we fear or despise and need to stereotype: Does the characterization of witches and stepmothers in folktales lead to stereotypes that harm such women? While an analysis of this question is beyond this study, history reflects wrongful persecution of women in the Salem Witch Trials. In 1692 Colonial America, hearings regarding so-called witchcraft in Salem, Massachusetts, sentenced about nineteen people to death and imprisoned countless others, based on stereotypical beliefs, coerced confessions, and accusations.[21] Folktales, myths, and film often demonize stepmothers and old, wise women; most pay homage to old seers and wise men. Some genres are more just. Some people are incapable of leading a righteous, just life; they are sociopaths and psychopaths, without conscience. Some have a conscience but choose to do wrong in order to advance their status and resources.

How does it apply to our lives? Living with people who tend to be destructive is a challenge. We can love them without liking them. Sometimes we have to disconnect and not associate with them for our health. We cannot control violent people. We are not responsible for their violent temperament, unless we are provoking trouble. If people grow up in a violent home, they are more likely to do violence. But with intervention from others, love, and commitment, we can overcome much of the earlier damage. What a tragedy that we fail to grasp the marvelous gifts of life and the great vulnerability of the human spirit.

THE SILENCE OF THE LAMBS

One of the most provocative and violent films of the late twentieth century is *The Silence of the Lambs*.[22] Jonathan Demme's film version of Thomas Harris's novel of the same name, a chilling, sinister psychological thriller and cinematographic sensation, won Academy Awards in five categories in 1992.[23] Jack Crawford (Scott Glenn), the head of the FBI's Behavioral Science Unit, selects a brilliant, young agent, Clarice Starling (Jodie Foster), to help save a missing woman from a psychopathic serial killer, "Buffalo Bill," who kidnaps, murders, and skins his young female victims. Buffalo Bill has kidnapped five women, keeping them up to three days before he kills them and takes some of their skin. Starling interviews an inmate of the Baltimore State Hospital for the criminally insane, Dr. Hannibal Lecter (Sir Anthony Hopkins), for insight into the killer's mind. Lecter is a brilliant, renowned psychiatrist turned infamous psychopathic, cannibalistic, serial killer. Crawford thinks Lecter—a clever mind manipulator—can help them locate the killer. For those like Lecter and Buffalo Bill, the category of human is not significant; they have no guilt, remorse, or concern that they are violence incarnate.

Lecter offers Starling a *quid pro quo*: he will only give Starling information if she supplies his morbid curiosity with details about her problematic life. They each delve deeply into the other's psyche. This convoluted relationship forces Starling to confront both her own demons and a demented, monstrous killer so powerful that she may not have the strength or the courage to stop him.

Hopkins, as Lecter, embodies and conveys "the charismatic essence of pure evil . . . a mixture of brilliant eloquence and inhuman cruelty . . . cultured gentleman and an unspeakable fiend."[24]

Foster owns the role of Clarice. Clarice, a rare fixture in thrillers—a female hero—becomes the film's human anchor over against the bizarre world of homicide, psychosis, and depravity. Starling faces the sexism and sexual politics that challenge a woman in a man's world. When undermined by male chauvinist cops, she escapes but then regroups and takes command. Starling champions victimized women and becomes a heroine.

The cold, calculating Lecter still desires to be seen as a human being, which draws him to Starling. He respects her intelligence, is intrigued by her ambition and femaleness, and is moved by her reminiscences of her past. By the end, both characters have had a profound impact upon each other. Conversely, Buffalo Bill, an ordinary demented personality drawn from Serial Killers 101, is a transvestite who is so fascinated with women that he creates an outfit out of their skin. Unfortunately, the movie fails to provide in-depth insight into his pathology. Lecter predicts Buffalo Bill will scalp his next victim, and Starling thinks Buffalo Bill wants to create a vest with victims' skins. When Bill's sixth victim is found, Starling and Crawford fly to West Virginia to investigate. They find a moth chrysalis in the victim's throat and triangular-shaped patches of skin removed. Starling believes Lecter knows Buffalo Bill's real identity.

Meanwhile, Buffalo Bill kidnaps Catherine Martin, the daughter of the junior U.S. senator from Tennessee, in Memphis. Crawford sends Starling to get more information from Lecter. They believe Lecter knows the true identity of Buffalo Bill. Starling bargains with Lecter: if his information leads to Buffalo Bill's arrest and saves Catherine Martin's life, Lecter will be transferred to a new institution, with more freedom. After Starling conveys more personal information, Lecter suggests that Bill obsesses about moths because of their metamorphosis. Lecter advises Starling to check on people with violent convictions who were rejected for gender reassignment surgery; James Gumb has a penchant for using his victims' skin to make an apron and is obsessed with butterflies and moths.

Chilton, the warden, who has tapped Lecter and Starling's conversation, knows that the deal is a lie. Chilton tells Lecter that if he reveals Buffalo Bill's identity, he will get a transfer to another asylum, if Chilton gets credit. Lecter will only give the information to Senator Martin in person, in Tennessee. Chilton consents. Lecter has made and hidden a handcuff key. Once he is outside the asylum, he will be in the custody of police officers who will use only handcuffs. In Tennessee, Lecter plays mind games with Senator Martin, but finally gives information about Buffalo Bill. The FBI goes to save Catherine.

Starling confronts Lecter because she thinks Lecter has misled everyone. They continue their quid pro quo dialogue,[25] but Chilton interrupts the conversation, preventing Lecter from telling her a parallel understanding of Buffalo Bill. Starling leaves, and that evening, Lecter escapes, kills both guards, eludes law enforcement, and gets to the airport in an ambulance.

Starling recognizes that Buffalo Bill's first victim was found third, insinuating that Bill wanted to hide her body, so she must have known Bill personally. Starling discovers that the first victim was a tailor; ergo, Buffalo Bill is a tailor who wants to become a woman by making himself a "woman suit" of real skin. They search records at Johns Hopkins showing that Gumb had been turned down for gender reassignment surgery. Starling goes to interview the victim's former employer, and Gumb answers the door. When she sees a Death's Head Moth, Gumb's signature, in the background, she knows she is face–to-face-with Buffalo Bill.

When she tries to arrest Gumb, he escapes to the basement. She follows. Starling sees that Catherine Martin is still alive. With the lights out, Bill slips up behind Starling and cocks his gun. Hearing the click, she fires back, killing him. Catherine Martin is rescued. Starling completes her FBI training. The movie ends as we see Lecter telephoning Starling following her graduation from the FBI Academy. Apparently on a Caribbean island, Lecter tells Starling he is "having an old friend for dinner" as his nemesis Chilton deplanes nearby. *The Silence of the Lambs* is a suspenseful thriller minus car crashes or chases, wild stunts, sex, gratuitous nudity, and blatant romance.

In this film, serial killers kill for the thrill of the hunt; the more macabre, the better. Buffalo Bill and Hannibal Lecter are vicious persons who do not value others. There are people in the world like them, with horrific pathologies. To them, people are merely pawns in a chess game of life. Theologically, it behooves us to teach people to discern when situations and people are not trustworthy. Trust should not be underrated. Further, it is important to learn how to live in community and work for justice. While we are not to control the lives of others, we are to respect each other, and not be controlled by those who cause harm. Can we love someone who can kill and cannibalize others? Such is the unconditional love of *agape*: to be able to love the most unlovable, while not condoning the despicable acts that they commit.

GRAND THEFT AUTO

In a most technological era, violence also occurs in video games. Video games involve players interacting with a computer-controlled virtual universe to achieve a goal or set of goals. In computer games, a video display is the basic feedback device. Of numerous popular games, one of the most lethal is *Grand Theft Auto* (GTA).

> Cross-legged on the floor, hands clutching the controls, 12-year-old Travis sits, engrossed in a video game. Eyes riveted to the television screen, he moves his fingers rapidly to make his character: (a) kill alien creatures invading earth, (b) survive the D-Day invasion at Normandy, or (c) have sex (usually out of sight, but signified by moans) with a woman, whom he then has the option of killing by various means. This is a worst-case scenario. Travis should not be able to buy violent and/or sexually explicit games. But they are out there.[26]

Grand Theft Auto, a computer and video game series which debuted in 1998, involves virtual crime. The player's goal is to advance up the ladder of criminal pursuits by engaging in acts of violence: kidnapping, assassination, stealing cars, running narcotics, and other criminal acts. The action takes place in three metropolitan areas: San Andreas (Los Angeles), Liberty City (Philadelphia), and Vice City (Miami). Each domain has a particular personality, and the authorities in each domain react differently to the player's action. To move about each city, one can use available public transportation or steal a car. One views the game from the top down as the camera zooms in and out, depending upon the particular scenario. The GTA games are best-sellers, and many leading screen actors have lent their voice-overs to the games, from Samuel L. Jackson and James Woods to Burt Reynolds, Dennis Hopper, and Miss Cleo.[27]

The games are violent, graphic, and have a great deal of sexual content, not appropriate for children under seventeen, according to the labels. The game design allows for engagement in a way that lets the players really immerse themselves in the game. For example, *GTA San Andreas* involves corruption, drugs, and gang violence. Set in Los Santos, one finds out that the mother of Carl Johnson has been murdered and the family subsequently has disintegrated. When two corrupt cops frame Johnson, he has to travel across San Andreas to regain control of the streets to save himself and his family. Johnson returns after having left the San Andreas neighborhood of Los Santos five years ago, when drugs and gang violence had been tearing the community apart. Johnson has more interactive aspects than previous GTA characters, from the capacity to swim and eat to survive, to working out at a gym and going to a gambling casino.[28]

GTA Vice City, set in the city of the same name, draws parallels from the television series *Miami Vice*, from the 1980s. This 2001 game, a smorgasbord of glamour, sex, and corruption, has enhanced effects: beautiful architecture, neon lights reflected on rain-slick streets, and intense Florida sunlight; the cars handle better, and pedestrians have a new crouch move. Vice City, with its beach, swamps, and ghetto, is a large, diverse, vibrant digital city. Vice City, a town of degradation and enchantment, is a major port of call with entrée to South America and the Caribbean. A social, friendly place, Vice City has lots of diverse characters—from real estate developers and politicians to athletes, pop stars, and migrants. Vice City crime boss, Sonny Forelli, sends ex-convict Tommy Vercetti to Vice City after Vercetti has finished serving time in a maximum security facility. When Vercetti arrives, things go badly: someone sets him up, and he has no money and no goods. Forelli wants his money back, but the Cuban gangsters, biker gangs, and corrupt politicians block him. Vercetti learns quickly that not only is trust rare, but that most of Vice City seems to want him dead, so he has to fight back and take over the city himself. The characters include crime lords with gold chains and bikini-clad women. Getaway cars move faster and the police are more intense, as minor offenses will increase the odds of the player being on the wanted list, and it will be more difficult for the player to get away. The player has a greater incentive to deal with the task at hand and not play around causing a commotion. The city layout is sophisticated with lots of fire escapes, backyards, and tiny alleys. There is a great deal of distinctive music, combat, voice acting, and neat clothes. GTA *Vice City*, with a lot of violence, has a compelling script and lots of opportunity for action.[29]

While some video games are educational and not violent, helping children learn logic, improving concentration, and encouraging thinking strategically, many of the new sophisticated video games are extremely violent: a woman may be a rape victim, and an attacker may urinate on her; females are often portrayed as hookers or sex toys: sexism personified. The attacker may have an option to kill her. Sometimes, there may be a sex scene, followed by the possibility of her murder, as in GTA *Vice City*. In some games, racism emerges as characters spout racial slurs. People tend to die amid screams, gore, and flying body parts.[30]

Though the *Entertainment Software Ratings Board* (ESRB) rated more than 1,026 games in 2004, giving 54 percent a rating of E or E10+ (for ages 10 and older), 33 percent a rating of T (for ages 13 and older), and 12 percent (including *Grand Theft Auto*) a rating of M (for ages 17 and older), one must be cautious about what children are allowed to view. Less than 1 percent got a rating of AO (for adults only). ESRB rates everything from alcohol to complexities of violence. In many of the videos there is a lot of blood and gore, rape, sexual assault, and foul language. Scientists note that they cannot verify that being exposed to simulated violence serves as a catalyst for youth criminal behavior. However, there seems to be a connection between violence and its effect on volatile youth, even if violence does not create unstable, violent youth. Caution remains the rule of the day. Medical and psychiatric professionals suggest that exposure to excessive violence in video games may desensitize children to violence, or they may believe the world is violent. Some argue that video games induce an ethos of disrespect and provoke aggressive behavior.[31] Regardless of one's perspective on video games, violence does not beget gentility; it begets more violence. Violence destroys, causes harm. Violence even snakes its way into theology and Christian dogma.

In sum, *Othello* shows us a phenomenal domestic tragedy that involves interpersonal and personal violence: deception, bigotry, envy, treachery, struggle, passion, and crime; relational violence, betrayal, and manipulation; race, class, and gender violence; scapegoating, violence, and heartache. Jealousy and mental illness can push a person over the edge to the extent that murder becomes a valid or optimum choice. In *The Bluest Eye*, Pecola, the main scapegoat, never experiences love, and in quest for it goes insane; she wanders around claiming her blue eyes. In *CSI*, the prominence of violence and death demonstrates the depths of cruelty that emerge when one has no sense of God consciousness, affording one the capacity to violate another in sickness, unto death. *Hansel and Gretel* reflect the violences of abandonment, cruelty, cannibalism, and new beginnings that can happen for people when they are no longer threatened by systemic oppression. *Grand Theft Auto* simulates virtual destruction and death, showing the depths to which businesses will go to package sensationalism for a profit. In life and narratives, people cause harm to others, they engage in violence, sometimes justifying their acts with Scripture.

Stories and tales of persons
Known and unknown
The rich and famous, the one made other
Each with a heart and a soul
Inspired, dynamic
Defiled, abused
Each one, ultimately
A fragile rose?

CHAPTER FOUR

VIOLENCE AND SYSTEMATIC THEOLOGY

The Bible, Shakespearean plays, and Grimm's fairy tales are best-selling books that are in many homes and schools. These books—their sacred, aesthetic, or family importance notwithstanding—are rife with stories about violence, though we usually do not think of them in this way. Modern bestsellers specializing in violence—"action"—mean huge profit, expenditures of financial resources by readers, and easy accessibility to pervasive violence-depicting sagas. Given the amount of violence contained in these historical texts, one has to wonder about their subliminal impact on readers and hearers. If we are not aware of the violence or we become anesthetized to its existence, what impact does this have on our bodies and psyches at a cellular level? I ask this question, rhetorically here, to emphasize again the vast amount of violence that saturates our cultural and religious realities. What would happen if we could eliminate some of this violence? Why is violence so appealing? Many books, films, and best-selling music CDs involve violence, often connected with sexual violence and abuse. The narratives we have examined demonstrate the proliferation of violence, the connections with popular culture and sexuality, and the theological connections to sacred and secular narratives.

Continuing with the driving questions for this volume—What is violence? What is the connection between violence and theology?—we now turn to explore the connections between violence and a particular, distinctive form of theology, systematic theology through a Womanist lens. One can approach the study of Christianity in several ways. Traditionally scholars studied Christianity in terms of historical categories: ancient and medieval, Scholastic, Reformation, the Enlightenment, neo-orthodox and postmodern (since the 1970s). Another option is to study Christianity in a topical manner, systematically. Scholars and theologians create systems or ways of studying theology wherein each category must be congruent with the other. One cannot say something in one category that contradicts another. These categories include: theology (study of God); Christology (study of Jesus Christ); soteriology (study of salvation); ecclesiology (study of the church); pneumatology (study of the Holy Spirit); hamartiology (study of sin); and anthropology (study of humanity). Christology in dialogue with atonement (soteriology) and theodicy are aspects of systematic theology where the violence is most evident and intriguing to me. The section on Jesus and violence in the New Testament reviewed the violence connected to Christology. I am intrigued that one who came as incarnated love, according to most traditions, had to be tortured and die to save the world. Why? Is the required sacrifice a matter of a maniacal, egocentric God, a Christ who needs to be a martyr, or is something else going on? How one understands Christology connects deeply with atonement. In Christian theology, atonement concerns reconciliation of humanity with God through the death of Christ. Christ is the lamb slain, the sacrifice made on behalf of humanity: a violent act occurs to redeem, or save, other people. Or, is there something else going on here? Whenever one speaks of violence, evil, or bad things happening, and I believe we can agree that crucifixion is a bad thing, the theological category is theodicy. Theodicy asks the question, How can bad things happen when God is good? The theodicy question goes to the heart of the "Why" question. Before resolving this conundrum, we first closely examine the definition of these critical terms.

Christology is the study of the Christ event—birth, life and teachings, death, and resurrection—and how those experiences affect the body of Christ, the church. The Christ event begins and comes to its penultimate climax in violence. As Mary carries the child, she is in danger of being the victim of violence. In ancient Israel, a woman betrothed and pregnant by someone other than her intended husband could be stoned (see Lev 20:10; Deut 22:20-22; John 8:3-7). But Joseph, her husband, as a righteous man, did not persecute Mary. How did she feel? What did she think, knowing what could have happened to her? Did she ever know fear, trepidation, and anxiety? From a Womanist perspective, Mary ultimately has no freedom; she is Joseph's property. Her society silences her concerns and gives her no voice. She does, however, transcend the role of property and becomes a subject as she proclaims the words of her Magnificat (Luke 1:46-55), where she acknowledges that God chose her to be *theotokos*, God-bearer. Joseph also embraces a point of liberation, for he accepts Mary without following his cultural normative practice of stoning her. With a word from God, Joseph, Mary, and child flee to Egypt to avoid a threat to their lives—the conspiracy by Herod (Matt 2:7-15). The dominant culture was oppressive to those deemed a threat to Herod, who heard about the birth of a new king; a new king was perceived as a threat. Scholars do not know of Jesus' movements and experiences after his encounter with the rabbis at the temple until John the Baptizer comes to baptize him, in the moment wherein God announces: *This is my Son* (Matt 3:13-17).

After the triumphal entry into Jerusalem on Palm Sunday (Matt 21), Jesus visits the temple, heals the lame and blind, and is quizzed about his authority. They taunt Jesus and ask him, "If he is Messiah, why does he not do something to change his circumstances?" (Matt 27:41-44). Judas, one of the disciples, betrays Jesus for the sum of thirty pieces of silver. When some Jews bring Jesus before Pilate, Pilate says he can find no fault in Jesus and washes his hands of the matter; though Pilate does not liberate Jesus. When given the opportunity, the crowd asks that the insurgent Barabbas be released and Jesus be crucified. Who are these people and why are they so against Jesus, the one they had honored and celebrated a week before? Why must Jesus suffer and die?

VIOLENCE AND THE ATONEMENT

Theologians and church tradition state that Jesus had to die for the sins of the world. They speak of Jesus as the worthy lamb who has been slain. René Girard has suggested that Jesus' crucifixion and resurrection expose the scapegoat. Yet, his theory states that one of the reasons why scapegoat theory works is that the scapegoat is hidden, has no power, and is a good pawn for the ills of others. If Girard is right, and the scapegoating of Jesus the Christ ends violence and sacrifice, why do we continue to do violence that results in death to life and death to spirit? Historically, there are several theories of atonement, which justify the mob violence and the state murder of Jesus. Atonement pertains to soteriology, or the doctrine of salvation. In Christian thought, salvation occurs through justification, which pertains to the crucifixion. Central to the faith is the belief that Jesus' suffering and death occur to secure salvation or reconciliation with God for humanity. That is, Jesus' death paid the price for human sin. There are many metaphors and basic theories of atonement.

Inna Jean Ray, in *The Atonement Muddle*,[1] does a historical analysis of atonement in which she stipulates the various ways we have understood atonement. During the Patristic Age (100–800 C.E.), there were many metaphors though no systematic theory of atonement: The metaphors of victory involved those over evil forces, ransom, redemption, and deliverance. Metaphors of divination included those of education and truth, by recapitulation, through glorification or exaltation; sacrifice; vicarious suffering and death; expiation of sins; and martyrdom. During the medieval period (1066–1500 C.E.) atonement theory emerged as salvation by justification. Anselm's (1033–1109) substitutionary theory argues that Christ's crucifixion offers retribution and satisfaction for human sin to God. Abelard's (1079–1142) subjective or moral influence theory of atonement claims that there is no universal human nature that dictates an original sin. Since, therefore, we do not "inherit" sin, people individually experience salvation through a one-on-one relationship with Christ, a relationship where love overcomes and transforms one's compulsion to sin or do wrong. With the Reformation, Grotius's (1583–1645) penal theory of atonement portrays the need to correct human fickleness and display divine wrathful power, which requires the punishment meted out by Christ. The Roman Catholic response via the Council of Trent (1545–1563) was a justification formula based on the incredible merits of Christ and the saints. During the periods of modernity and postmodernity, the primary atonement theories pertained to salvific liberation or rescue. Friedrich Schleiermacher (1768–1834) rejected atonement theory in lieu of a God consciousness where one experiences salvation as a type of interior growth. Albrecht Ritschl (1822–1889) rejected substitutionary atonement and opted for the new relationships that arise with the salvation revealed via Christ, through the Holy Spirit. Walter Rauschenbusch (1861–1918) supported a social gospel soteriology where the ministry, life, and preaching of Jesus is central and deals with the crucifixion as a matter of social realities and consequences. A backlash to World War I found the neo-orthodox school of thought, particularly via Karl Barth (1886–1968), with a return to atonement theory and the power of the revelation in Jesus Christ. For many so-called mainline churches and many nondenominational mega-churches in the twenty-first century, atonement theory is central to one's experience of conversion.

Womanist theologian Delores Williams[2] counters traditional atonement theories by positing that we should embrace the ministerial vision of Jesus Christ, which does not require blood, suffering, and the cross, where she uses Hagar as the metaphor for the surrogacy role of Black women. Karen Baker-Fletcher offers a Womanist, process relational, trinitarian view of atonement that understands Jesus the Christ is the one who brings freedom, deliverance, healing, and liberation for the poor, amid the paradox of the cross, using the metaphor of dance. In Christian tradition, God overcomes evil and death on the cross through the resurrection, yet our world continues to produce evil, death, and destruction. Baker-Fletcher argues that ransom-type atonement theories are erroneous, for God could never owe anything to Satan. Further, in the power of the Holy Spirit, through the risen Christ, people experience freedom from oppression, suffering, and abuse. Given his sociocultural context, the crucifixion of Jesus was inevitable, in that Jesus advocates on our behalf. Jesus was killed because he confronted the oppression in the violence-ridden society of his times. Baker-Fletcher contends that suffering is not redemptive, God's empathy in Christ is redemptive, where God overcomes evil and God offers humanity forgiveness: a profound, emphatic "No" to evil.[3]

When I reflect on many theories of Western Christology and atonement from a Womanist perspective, they seem problematic and fraught with concepts that, if taken to their logical conclusion, result in our glorifying suffering instead of salvation and transformation. Many of the hymns and recent praise songs of the Christian church valorize the cross and blood sacrifice. Being "washed in the blood" symbolizes for many salvation in and of itself. Yet, if we review the four accounts of the passion in the Gospels, noting the activities of the Passover meal, which then becomes the institution of the Last Supper—Jesus does not say *remember my death*, he says *remember me*. Yet within Christianity, most traditions have reduced or collapsed the Passover meal and the crucifixion into one ritual. So many of us glorify the suffering and death of Christ to the point that resurrection seems to get lost in the ritual drama, which frames the lives of Christians in a language that implies the suffering is final, that Easter seems to have no place in the Eucharist (the Lord's Supper, Holy Communion). This thought seems to get concretized even more so with the presence of the most significant symbol of Christianity: the cross, the place where Jesus was crucified.

Crucifixion was deemed the most humiliating death one could experience at the time of Jesus. When one lifts up the cross to such heights—worn around one's neck, mounted atop churches, and hung in prominent places and spaces in church sanctuaries—do we not glorify and worship suffering and therefore practice idolatry? Have we missed the essence of Jesus' teaching? Or, is wearing the cross irony? Do we take a symbol of shame and elevate it to a symbol of honor? Are we successful, or have we used the cross in such a way that we have become anesthetized to its violence and to the many ways in which we are complicit in everyday violence? Jesus does not wear a cross; he only gives witness to Abba, to our Creator as worthy of worship. Jesus never says *worship me*. In worshiping Jesus, do we somehow obliterate the full experience of the three-in-one Godhead? Are we violating the covenants with the biblical God and are we in opposition to what we are confessing when we pray the Lord's Prayer? That is, if we fixate on the cross and suffering, is this not the antithesis of being delivered from evil and embracing the command to love God with all our hearts and love our neighbors as ourselves? A Womanist lens reminds us to ask the hard questions, recognizing that we may not have all of the answers as we intentionally unmask issues pertaining to oppression.

Atonement or becoming "at-one" with God means being reconciled with God, where notions of power and authority on heaven and earth are critical. Those who tend to be oppressed are those in a given society without power. Glorifying suffering does not empower those who do not have power. One option is to recognize the historicity of Jesus' suffering, death, and resurrection, while focusing on the dynamics of love and justice that Jesus taught. Embodying love and justice in community eliminates the need to oppress others, as persons have power *with*, rather than power *over*. The misuse of power and acts of oppression amid the problem of justice has troubled theologians since time immemorial. Justice continues to be a problem today, in a world fraught with systematic classism, sexism, and racism—denying access because of what they look like, where they have come from, and their particular socioeconomic status, the problem of theodicy.

VIOLENCE AND THEODICY

People who believe in God have to deal with the problem of theodicy; that is, how we can affirm the reality of a good, unlimited powerful God of justice and see the incredible depths of evil and violence on a daily basis. For an atheist or for believers in philosophies and other types of spiritualities, theodicy is not an issue but rather a kind of karma, destiny, or part of chaos. Traditionally, philosophers have wrestled with the issue of God and evil by asking if God exists, with the following theories as options: non-being, dualism, despotism, and moral theory.[4] Scottish philosopher and historian David Hume expressed the question accordingly:

> Is God willing to prevent evil, but not able? Then God is impotent. Is God able to prevent evil, but not willing? Then God is malevolent. Is God both willing and able to prevent evil? Then why is there any evil in the world?[5]

Most Anglo-American analytic philosophers tend to build a theodicy based on St. Augustine's (354–430 C.E.) free will defense or Irenaeus's (130–202 C.E.) progressive human perfection theory.[6]

Augustine of Hippo insisted that human freedom exists, but that it is ensnared in sin. Because God is good and sovereign and everything God created is good, and evil exists (due to the Fall), God must have allowed evil for some good reason.[7] Within this framework, Augustine presents a free will argument. God knows everything but does not thwart human freedom. Evil is the opposite of good. God is the greatest Good. Since evil is the turn from God, the source of sin is rooted in the mystery of finite freedom.[8]

Irenaeus, Bishop of Lyon, claimed God is an involved creator, and the ultimate link of God's activity with humanity is in Jesus Christ. Irenaeus builds his theodicy by showing the difference between the "image" and the "likeness" of God in human beings. The *imago*, in a person's bodily form, epitomizes human nature as a lucid creature with the capacity to fellowship with her or his

Creator. God's likeness in humanity represents the ultimate perfecting (moving toward wholeness, holiness, completion) of humanity by the Holy Spirit.[9] The Holy Spirit perfects an individual and makes her or him in the "image" *and* "likeness" of God. Without perfection, a person has the *imago* (moral freedom and responsibility) of God, but not the likeness (reflecting the Creator's essence). Human beings are born undeveloped, unsuited for receiving highest divine gifts.

God can do all things, but created order must be inferior to God; for God created that order, and God has always existed. For Irenaeus, God is compassionate and sees that sin sprang from Adam and Eve's imperfections, their frailty and vulnerability. God's revelation in history and God's need for human response in faith guarantee human freedom. God places the will and control of human freedom with human beings. God's Son, Jesus Christ, experiences childhood so that humanity may receive the Son.[10] In sum, Augustine argues for a free will defense and a fall doctrine, with broken humanity. Irenaeus argues for soul-making and the spiritual and moral development of immature creatures, amid divinely appointed good and evil toward God's perfection and good purpose.

Contemporary philosopher John Hick (1922–) chose the Irenean path of theodicy and develops a "soul-making" model. A soul-making theodicy places evil at the center of an environment where God shapes souls that grow into perfect relationship with God. Human beings are created gradually in the image of God, granting the possibility of personal relationship, character development, and fellowship with God. Hick's developmental, eschatological, teleological theodicy evolves and expects the results of and the answers to the mystery of evil in the future.[11] Hick notes that the results of this process depend on seeing moral evil and suffering in relation to God's will revealed in Christ Jesus.

Kenneth Surin (1948–), a philosopher and theologian, however, criticizes the traditional focus on method of most philosophers and theologians, and says that studying canonical or classical theodicy, as a theoretical and nonhistorical activity, frustrates historically and counts against a just Christian reply to the *problem of evil.*[12] Surin's stress on the historicity and contingency of language, culture, and theology highlights the problems of traditional theodicy; and he notes that for some horrible evils, theodicy has no solution. He respects the depths and complexity of God, evil, and story as an interwoven tapestry with patterns of epistemological crises, suffering, and redemption through messianic praxis. Unfortunately, Surin never defines what messianic praxis is. Suffice it to say, the terminology implies that we live our daily lives circumscribed by our experience of the Messiah, though this is interpretation of a powerful phrase left ambiguous.

In my Womanist analysis of the African American Spirituals,[13] the question of theodicy was central to my research. African American Spirituals are chants of collective exorcism; songs the slaves used in this country to name and subvert their lived realities. They created these songs in community, in response to their total realities; for coming out of African traditions, they did not see a separation between the so-called secular and sacred; all existence is of God. I sang these songs all of my life, discovered them as marvelous illustrative materials for teaching music pedagogy, and rediscovered them during my doctoral program, and they became my primary subject for my dissertation. Howard Thurman, Martin Luther King, Jr., and James Cone create thematic, biblical liberation and community-based views of theodicy from an African American perspective that takes community and the Spirituals seriously.

Howard Thurman (1900–1981), mystic, theologian, pastor, and ecumenist, proposed the idea of community, "the search for common ground" as a goal for all life and the basis for ethical reflection.[14] Liberty is an exterior privilege, option, or grant that a social entity gives an individual. Community, as achieved potential, concerns wholeness, harmony, and integration. The self, God, and the world shape community. Suffering concerns the personalized problem of evil and hostile activity toward God.[15] Thurman posits that all evil is redemptive, even innocent suffering.[16] For Thurman, the question posed by theodicy is to determine what we do with that which affects us privately for good or bad, and how we stop evil from destroying all meaning in human lives. In response, Thurman states that one does everything within one's power to arrest evil, and replaces the evil with something good, by internalizing love and truth and then by working to perfect love and truth in society. One says "No!" to evil because the community's work is the Work of God.[17]

Martin Luther King, Jr. (1929–1968), minister, civil rights activist, apostle of nonviolence, and Nobel Prize winner, begins his theological and ethical discussion with a search for "the beloved community." He saw nonviolent direct action as the solution to overcome the barriers to community on a domestic and international level.[18] *The beloved community*, a Christian social eschatological ideal, is a mutual, voluntary, cooperative experience that affirms solidarity and embraces relationships among people, God, and the world. King asserted the ultimate goodness, the sacredness of all humanity, for all are created *imago Dei, made free.* The daily work of living a balanced life produces the likelihood of sin.[19] God, the rational, loving Purposer in history, sustains and creates life as a just God. For King, one must pursue community in unity with God, despite the barriers of sin and evil. God reveals divine purposes through the Christ event; and people acting as free, self-directed, and self-conscious participants cooperate intimately with God to create community. King sees Christ as the model and source for the beloved community; the Cross symbolizes God's redemptive love. Thus theodicy concerns God's limiting divine power to allow for human responsibility and freedom.[20] God does not cause evil, but permits evil to protect human freedom. Cooperation with God against evil is the way to overcome evil. King's beloved community is the model for life in all areas, from civil rights to world peace. Agape, ultimate love, allows one to be a good neighbor and to engage in forgiveness and reconciliation. *The beloved community* includes a loving, just God and a balanced life rooted in the love of one's neighbor, self-respect, and the power to choose. King's view of sin shows how widespread individual and communal evil can be.

James Cone, systematic and Black liberationist theologian,[21] was the first scholar to develop a theological understanding of what Black power means to Black religious people: Black power is Christ's central message to twentieth-century America. Black power means the absolute freedom and release of Black people from white oppression by any means African Americans find necessary. Black power meant freedom now, Black self-determination, and choosing to die standing up rather than to live while kneeling.[22] Cone distinguished between Black hatred and Black power. Black hatred was the African American's disgust with and dislike of Eurocentric society. African Americans needed a sense of self-worth about Blackness. Black power meant hope and freedom for African Americans, with the ability to choose.[23]

Cone's model for theodicy is liberation. Jesus, the center of Christianity, is a liberator with the message of Black power. Jesus, within the gospel of the oppressed, makes Christianity compatible with Black power. Christianity and Black power proclaim freedom: when one sees the fulfillment of her or his being and can help materialize that vision. Black power can help shoulder these risks and help people live freely. God's righteousness means God creates freedom, does justice, vindicates the poor, loves and acts on behalf of humanity, but does not condone evil. One reconciles Black power with the loving gospel of Jesus Christ. God's love affirms Black people and moves them to confront the white neighbor. Justice tempers love to make human relationships meaningful. Black power wants to meet the needs of the oppressed in love as the work of the Holy Spirit. The task of Black theology presses for a new comprehension of Black dignity among Black people towards dissolving white racism: transformational theodicy. Black theology must ultimately address Black suffering, as a social, political, theological, functional, "this worldly" living reality.[24] Thus, Cone develops a theodicy that talks about meaningful relationships with God and humanity, where both the oppressed and those who oppress experience transformation and empowerment. In asking whether God cares, Thurman, King, and Cone, three Black theologians, looked specifically to the Spirituals for answers.[25]

Howard Thurman's search for *the common ground* expressed the question of theodicy concerning how people handle issues affecting them privately, and how they stop evil from destroying all meaning in human life. For Thurman, the Spirituals chronicle the slaves' experience of suffering and their identity with Jesus, proffering a universal gift of liberation. Martin Luther King, Jr.'s search for *the beloved community* led him toward the question of theodicy as he claimed that God limits divine power to allow human freedom and human responsibility. The Spirituals are metaphors for King's own vision and faith, and allow him to view the dialectics of good and evil, optimism and pessimism, hope and apathy, and affirmation and pain. James Cone's exegesis or critique of Black Power supports a theodicy that champions immediate freedom, Black self-determination, and the right to choose. Cone argues that the *Spirituals* do not raise questions about God's existence or matters of theodicy. In sum, the *Spirituals* record the suffering and Jesus' gift of liberation for Thurman; provide symbols of personal vision, faith, and the dialectical nature of the spiritual, physical, and ethical life for King; and provide documents of confession, resistance, and theology to address human salvation as power for Cone.

Listening to Spirituals, these chants of collective exorcism, singing them, studying their sociohistorical, cultural, aesthetic backgrounds allowed me to "hear" them in a way, such that the Spirituals themselves told me how to analyze them. Beginning with the context, or sociohistorical analysis, the work of René Girard and his mimetic, scapegoat theory helped to unmask the troubles and tensions, the double bind, and bolstered the morale, moral wisdom, and hope of slave bards, and later civil rights activists during the 1960s civil rights movement. Second, the work of W. E. B. Du Bois provided the tools to explore the paradoxes and tensions within the stories, the narrative-dialectic: the double consciousness. Third, analyzing the texts of the lyrics and the music through the notion of signifying, reflected in work by Henry Louis Gates, Jr., provided the lens to see the creative spirit, the double voicing of these songs. Fourth, the tremendous faith and thought emanating from the Spirituals, or the philosophical-theological analysis, came to life via the concepts of philosopher Martin Buber, with his concept of double relations, "I-Thou, I-It."

These interdisciplinary categories formed the basic structure of my Womanist analysis of the Spirituals.

My Womanist, interdisciplinary analysis asked numerous questions about context, story, creative spirit, and faithful thought. The answers arising from these songs hewn in community are rich, powerful, and transformative. The bards who created, sang, and transmitted the more than 6,000 Spirituals, according to James Lovell, Jr., were clear that they were slaves physically, but not spiritually and mentally. Their enslavement was not a punishment by God, and was not a state in life they deserved. The Spirituals helped the slaves have an eschatology that allowed them to live through oppression and slavery, without succumbing to its evils. Their relationships with God and with one another allowed them surreptitiously to name the racist pathology, indicting the slave owners, without bringing harm to the slaves themselves. They were able to signify, using language in a coded fashion where the outsider (dominant culture) would hear the words and music and think the slaves were content and humble. The slave bards, and their later progeny, the civil rights workers, would sing these songs naming the wrong while empowering themselves to seize the means available to them to right the wrongs of slavery and racism. Thus they could sing "Steal Away to Jesus," and depending upon the particular context, could be sending a message that the Underground Railroad was passing or that there would be a prayer meeting in their gathering place or, for some, this was a desire to return to the ship named "Jesus" that brought them, stolen and in shackles from the African continent, so they could return home.

Slaves knew an intimacy with God, connected with the revolutionary Jesus and related to Christian symbols, but not the hypocrisy, self-righteousness, and original sin of the U.S. civil religion of racism and enslaving others. The slaves wanted freedom and empowerment; they were not in denial about their heinous contextual experiences of slavery. Yet, they were clear about God and justice in the Spirituals. The Spirituals reflect their soul theology, wherein their core beliefs helped them survive and heal: a theology of grace, justice, and ultimate power. Their understanding of Jesus was a sense of goal-orientation of right relations. Human choice, greed, the capacity to objectify others, and the need to exploit and control caused slavery. Neither slavery nor racism derived from God's judgment. Slaves claimed freedom for themselves in the present, though they might not have an immediate experience. Thus, the Spiritual "I Got Shoes" affirmed that even though many slaves had no shoes, they could envision a time when their children would have shoes, the shoes of freedom, respect, and dignity.

Interestingly, with the quest for freedom from racist injustice during the antebellum and 1960s civil rights eras, many did not focus on gender injustice, though men and women together were being oppressed. Sadly, even today, many in dominant culture deny racism. Many in global culture deny the reality and impact of sexism and classism. The Black woman's voice, agency, and feelings about the problem of evil and God has been omitted in contemporary theological and general scholarly reflection until the emergence of Womanist[26] scholarship. Kelly Delaine Brown-Douglas, theologian and Episcopal priest, states that many Black female writers and scholars recognized that although male-centered Black theology laid the groundwork for new theologies, the limits of this male-centered Black theology meant it could not help Black women articulate and think through Black women's and Black men's labors to "make do and do better."[27] And, thus it is a Womanist, interdisciplinary analysis that says we can no longer deny the presence of evil and violence in our world, in our religious and secular lives in every arena, including race, gender, class and poverty, sexual orientation, and mental and physical disabilities. "Denial is not a river in Egypt," and pretending that Christianity as practiced is pristine and without violence is hypocrisy and arrogance personified. Like Howard Thurman and Delores S. Williams, perhaps we need to go back to the Gospels, and prayerfully discern what it really means to be a follower of Jesus the Christ.

CONCLUSION

There is no place in the world that one can go—no country, place, religious order, or governmental structure—where violence does not have deep roots. In secular and religions arenas, violence is there. As a global village, we have not done a good job at loving the neighbor—our neighbor within ourselves, our faith or secular communities. We use the excuses of difference to assault others. Our need to acquire power gives us permission to access greed, to manipulate, disrespect, and control others. We control and abuse ourselves and others through actions and words. With the presence of weapons of mass destruction or lack thereof, one of our greatest weapons is our tongue. What we say, how we say it, and when we say it is often incredibly devastating. Our fear of others, fear of difference, and our insecurities allow us to embrace unnecessary violence as an option. Violence seems to be inherent to the very fabric of most cultures in the world. Before we can ever change anything with the preponderance of violence, we must admit that it exists. We must name it and claim our participation before we can transform violence and create a better world. The question remains, are we up for it, or would we rather pretend our existence is a game of virtual reality?

There are many options available to help us transform our world. First, we ought to become good students of history, geography, and culture. If we do not know the global stories of colonization, how evangelism was often more culturally based than religious, how many wars have been fought and lives lost in the name of religion and imperialism, we will continue to make the same mistakes. We must understand that every life is important, every life lost to unnecessary violence is a travesty, whether that life is one who will never travel beyond a ten-mile radius of her or his home or that life is a head of state. Second, it is important to be aware of current events, social culture, economic realities, and systemic oppression; to understand global systems of power and control, so that we can make wise, ethical choices. Third, all children should have courses in conflict resolution starting about third grade. Part of the reason we get into trouble is that we have not learned how to agree to disagree, how to compromise and work through issues in mature, healthy ways. Fourth, when thinking about our lives, it is crucial to avoid compartmentalizing parts of our lives so that we have a schizophrenic as opposed to an integrative, whole existence. Fifth, in creating religious education that involves everything from sermons to matters of family life, we need to be sensitive about the power of language and the power and complexity of the Bible. Instead of teaching people selective readings of the text and using the excuse of "it's in the Bible" to press our agendas, we need to invite people to ask questions about what is in the Bible, to learn biblical history, archaeology, and anthropology so that we can understand how there are times when twenty-first century questions are not always answered by ancient texts. Sixth, it is important to understand that in the twenty-first century, when it comes to brokering power, having the majority of the resources and positions of authority and control, this is still a man's world; when it comes to those who are most oppressed, most vulnerable, most disregarded and exploited, it is the world of women and people of color. Until we tell the truth about this skewed panorama, we can never hope to begin to effect change and limit the amount of violence that occurs on a daily basis. Seventh, all persons are created in God's image, persons to be respected. Respect for self and others is foundational for being a good steward of one's gifts, graces, and resources; for developing holistic and cultural health that support survival and thriving of individuals and communities. A spiritual ethos of wellness involves creating individual and communal attitudes of gratitude with the capacity to share, in being *with* as opposed to being *against* or being *over* in a punitive way. Awareness of life as gift helps to instill such an attitude. Awareness of what it means to be a responsible being in relationship to other sentient beings and all of nature is to be accountable, in everything from not being wasteful to taking time to appreciate the dynamics of what it means to be a human *being*, not a human *doing*. Participation in community requires acceptance about the potential and limitations of being human, recognizing that one cannot always be right and recognizing the gift of forgiveness so that pain and hurt from the past does not have to control us. Awareness of the dynamics of life, the importance of total health, and the devastation of unnecessary violence calls us to embrace a vibrant, integrative theology with responsive ethics. Violence does not have to overwhelm our world; yet choices have been made so that it does. Only when enough people globally get sick and tired of being sick and tired, and have the courage to sit together with shared power and compromise, can we hope to become more conscious of the violence and decide to live our lives differently. If we fail to make some changes, we may not have to worry about getting along, because we will destroy each other, desecrate the planet, and the world will cease to be as we know it.

A butterfly, a song, a baby's smile
Creation, radiant; life, vital
Can we get along?
Do we want to get along?
What are we afraid of?
Do we care about God?
How God must weep
At our careless disregard.

NOTES

INTRODUCTION

1. All poetry in this volume is by the author.

1. LANDSCAPE OF VIOLENCE

1. "New WHO report presents more complete picture of global violence," http://www.who.int/mediacentre/news/releases/pr73/en/.

2. Karen Baker-Fletcher, *Dancing with God: The Trinity from a Womanist Perspective* (St. Louis, Mo: Chalice Press, 2006), 38.

3. See René Girard, *The Scapegoat; To Double Business Bound; Things Hidden at the Beginning of the World; The Girard Reader* (ed. James G. Williams; New York: Crossroad, 1996); *Curing Violence* (ed. Theophus Smith and Mark I. Wallace; Sonoma, Cal.: Polebridge Press, 1994).

4. Theophus Smith, "King and the Black Religious Quest to Cure Racism," in *Curing Violence*, 248-49.

5. Gil Bailie, "Cinema and Crisis: The Elusive Quest for Catharsis," *Image* 20 (1998): 17-20. For example, in Alice Walker's novel *The Color Purple*, Celie is Mr. ___'s scapegoat. He abuses her in a variety of ways over time. Shug, Celie, and Mr. ___ form a mimetic triangle. Both Celie and Mr. ___ desire Shug. When the triangle collapses and tension mounts between Celie and Mr. because Celie realizes that Mr. ___ has been keeping her children's letters from her, and that she no longer has to take the abuse, Celie would have tried to kill Mr. ___ had it not been for Shug intervening. What do we do when we identify violence and see others doing wrong? Do we rid the community of all violence, conflict, and stress by blaming all wrongdoing on one individual, or do we educate the community as to its own complicity?

6. Conversations with Diana Culbertson, Professor of Literature, Kent State University, Summer, 1995. Stoning to death is the ancient world's equivalent.

7. For more in-depth discussion on scapegoating, see Cheryl Kirk-Duggan, *Misbegotten Anguish: Theology and Ethics of Violence* (St. Louis: Chalice Press, 2001).

8. Ronald Austin, "Sacrificing Images: Violence and the Movies," *Image* 20 (1998): 23-25.

9. http://www.who.int/mediacentre/news/releases/pr73/en/.

10. http://www.childrensdefense.org at the press page.

11. Kimberly Svevo, UNESCO: "Global Report on Child Abuse and Neglect." Cited December 1998. http://www.unesco.org/webworld/child_screen/documents/kimberley.rtf. "UN: Internet Porn is Fuelling Child Abuse," *Asian Sex Gazette.* Cited 16 November 2004. Online: http://www.asiansexgazette.com/asg/southeast_asia/southeast03news11.htm.

12. Max Taylor and John Horgan, eds., *The Future of Terrorism* (London: Frank Cass, 2000); Social science definition, Alex P. Schmid, "Terrorism and the Use of Weapons of Mass Destruction" in *Where the Risk?* 128-29 (n. 18), 3-6.

13. Lee Griffith, *The War on Terrorism and the Terror of God* (Grand Rapids, Mich.: Wm. B. Eerdmans, 2002), 6-8.

14. Ibid., 37-74.

15. Ibid., 79-128.

16. Ibid., 214.

17. Robert E. Hood, *Begrimed and Black: Christian Traditions on Blacks and Blackness* (Minneapolis: Fortress, 1994), 91-96, 117.

18. Stephen R. Haynes, *Noah's Curse: The Biblical Justification of American Slavery* (New York: Oxford University Press, 2002).

19. The Commission on Faith and Order and the Program to Combat Racism and *Racism in Theology; Theology Against Racism* (Geneva: World Council of Churches, 1975), 1-4, 5, 6, 13-15.

20. Bernard Braxton, *Sexual, Racial and Political Faces of Corruption* (Washington, DC: Verta Press, 1977), 7-8, 13-16, 19-24.

21. "Women in a Dangerous World: No Place for Your Daughters," *The Economist.* Cited 24 November 2005. Online: Women's Human Rights Net. http://www.whrnet.org/docs/issue-dangerous-0512.htm. In many ways we are not that far removed from the times when women were considered the property of their fathers or their husbands. Thus any acts of violence against such women were considered property damage done to the man, not a personal attack on the woman.

22. "Facts and Figures on VAW." Online: http://www.unifem.org/gender_issues/violence_against_women.

23. Kirk-Duggan, *Misbegotten Anguish*, 66-67.

24. George Allan, "Conservatives, Liberals, and the Colonized: Ontological Reflections," *Process Studies* 23 (Winter 1994): 256, 257, 268, 269; see Albert Memmi, *The Colonizer and the Colonized*, trans. Howard Greenfeld [Portrait du colonisé précédé du portrait du colonisateur, Corrêa: Editions Buchet/Chastel, 1957] (Boston: Beacon Press, 1967), 120.

25. See John Rawls, *Justice as Fairness: A Restatement* (Cambridge, Mass.: Belknap Press, 2001).

26. Michael Walzer, *Spheres of Justice: A Defense of Pluralism and Equality* (New York: Basic Books, 1983).

27. Robert Nozick, *Anarchy, State, Utopia* (New York: Basic Books, 1977).

28. Alice Walker, *In Search of Our Mothers' Gardens: Womanist Prose* (New York: Harcourt Brace Jovanovich, 1983), xi.

2. SKETCHES OF VIOLENCE IN THE BIBLE

1. There is a Jewish and Christian canon, and the books vary. The Christian canon includes the Old Testament and New Testament. Some versions of the Christian Bible include books from the Apocrypha, additional books written during the time of other accepted Scriptures, but not included in the Christian canon. Note that there are three versions of the Ten Commandments: Jewish, Catholic, and Protestant.

2. Leon Kass, "Farmers, Founders, and Fratricide: The Story of Cain and Abel," *First Things* 62 (April 1996): 19-26. Online: http://www.leaderu.com/ftis ues/ft9604/articles/kass.html. Kass notes that while God did not accept Cain's sacrifice, God did not reject it. Cain's reactions involve a violence of his own person: anger, shame, and wounded pride—the acknowledgment of some of the first human emotions. God's unenthusiastic response to Cain's offering results in Cain feeling slighted, which he probably then transfers to Abel, who God seemed to favor to Cain's chagrin: sibling rivalry. God's mysterious message to Cain seems to imply that if Cain does well, he will receive acceptance. Cain feels like Abel's success is Abel's playing one-upsmanship. The bitterness of not having his own gift respected is nothing compared with that of seeing the greater success of his lesser brother. Cain treats Abel's success in sacrifice as if Abel had been trying to outdo him. God's advice to Cain about "doing well" and its opposite are available and make sense to human beings, without further direction. Genesis 3 indicates that human beings do have some kind of knowledge of good and bad. Cain engages in premeditated murder, probably out of jealousy, ridding himself of his key rival.

3. Danna Nolan Fewell, "Judges," in *Women's Bible Commentary* (ed. Carol A. Newsom and Sharon H. Ringe; Louisville: John Knox/Westminster, 1992, 1998), 73-83.

4. The others include Jezebel and her daughter Athaliah: Jezebel persecutes and murders God's prophets (1 Kgs 16:31; 18:4-19; 19:1-2; 21:5-25); and Athaliah kills or has killed all males of her court, including her offspring; though unknown to her, one grandchild, Jehoash, is rescued (2 Kgs 8:26; 11:1-20). In the apocryphal book bearing her name, Judith, with her maid in collusion, decapitates Holofernes, a general of Nebuchadnezzar, to protect her town of Bethuliah (Jdt 13: 6-8). Herodias and her daughter Salome cause the decapitation of John the Baptizer (Matt 14:1-12).

5. Philip A. Cunningham, "The Arrest and Sentencing of Jesus: A Historical Reconstruction," *Journal of Religion and Society* Vol 6 (2004). Online at http://moses.creighton.edu/jrs/2004/2004-8.html.

6. Anne Catherine Emmerich, *The Dolorous Passion of Our Lord Jesus Christ* (Rockford, Ill.: T A N Books & Publishers; Repr. 1994).

7. John T. Pawlikowski, "Christian Anti-Semitism: Past History, Present Challenges," *Journal of Religion and Society* Vol. 6 (2004). Online at http://moses.creighton.edu/jrs/2004/2004-10.html; Ched Myers, *"The Passion:* The Gospel as Political Parody," *The Witness Magazine;* online at http://thewitness.org/agw/myers040704.html.

8. See Mark 14–15; Matthew 26–27; Luke 22–23; John 18–19; Cunningham, "The Arrest and Sentencing of Jesus."

9. Cunningham, "The Arrest and Sentencing of Jesus."

10. From the Declaration on the Relation of the Church to Non-Christian Religions, *Nostra Aetate* 4, in Michael G. Lawler, "Sectarian Catholicism and Mel Gibson," *Journal of Religion and Society* Vol. 6 (2004). Online at http://moses.creighton.edu/jrs/2004/2004-6.html.

11. William D. Edwards, Wesley J. Gabel, Floyd E. Hosmer, "On the Physical Death of Jesus Christ," JAMA Vol 255, No. 11 (March 21, 1986), 1456. Accessed online at http://www.godandscience.org/apologetics/deathjesus.pdf.

12. It is unclear in this Gospel what the "crowd" is. In some riots, a "crowd" has less than a half-dozen participants.

13. Ched Myers notes that concerning the question of Jesus' arrest as a robber in Mark 14, the biblical allusion probably pertains to the arrest of the prophet Jeremiah (Jeremiah 37:13). According to the ancient philosopher Josephus, the Greek term "leesteen," which describes "social bandits," may include "Robin hood-type urban terrorists," "rural insurgents," or "nationalist Jewish guerillas." Mark then views Jesus as being arrested as an insurrectionist. "If modern readers (or filmmakers) wish to ignore or deny the political character of Jesus' ministry, they must assert that these officials misunderstood their prisoner—which flies in the face of the plain meaning of the narrative." Myers, *"The Passion:* The Gospel as Political Parody."

14. "But then, in a shrewd public relations ploy aimed at playing the unruly crowd's patriotism off against itself, [Pilate] decides to defuse the possibility of a popular uprising by granting a special, festival-specific amnesty ([Mark] 15:6) . . . . 'Barabbas' (whose name translates ironically as 'son of the father') is then introduced into the narrative as someone 'who had committed murder in the insurrection' (15:7). By this Mark likely means [Barabbas] was a Sicarii operative, insurgents who were known for political assassinations." Ibid.

15. Myers, *"The Passion:* The Gospel as Parody."

16. Edwards, Gabel, and Hosmer, "On the Physical Death of Jesus Christ," 1456-58. Accessed online at http://www.godandscience.org/apologetics/deathjesus.pdf. The material in this paragraph is drawn from this article.

17. Ibid., 1460.

18. For a discussion of the phrase "Son of Man" and its meaning, see Carl Holladay, *A Critical Introduction to the New Testament: Interpreting the Message and Meaning of Jesus Christ* (Nashville: Abingdon, 2005), 117-18.

19. For a brief introduction to these issues, see Raymond E. Brown, *An Introduction to the New Testament* (New York: Doubleday, 1997), 166-67.

20. Jerusalem was unusually crowded because the feast of Passover was taking place.

3. SKETCHES OF VIOLENCE IN CULTURAL NARRATIVES

1. William Shakespeare, *Othello* (New York: Signet Classics; revised edition, 1998); http://absoluteshakespeare.com/guides/othello/summary/othello_summary.htm.

2. Toni Morrison, *The Bluest Eye* (New York: Penguin/PLUME, 1970).

3. Ibid., 47.

4. Ibid., 165; his name is Soaphead Church (because of his hair style and his training for ministry), aka Elihue Micah Whitcomb—"Celibacy [is his] haven, silence a shield."

5. Ibid., 172.

6. Ibid., 173-76.

7. Ibid., 172-73.

8. Phyllis Klotman, "Dick-and-Jane and the Shirley Temple Sensibility in *The Bluest Eye*," *Black American Literature Forum* 13 (1979): 123-25.

9. Morrison, *Bluest Eye*, 39.

10. Ibid., 38-39.

11. Ibid., 110, 111.

12. Ibid., 39.

13. Ibid., 42.

14. Rosalie Baum, "Alcoholism and Family Abuse in *Maggie* and *The Bluest Eye*," *Mosaic* 19 (Summer 1986): 99; Denise Heinze, *The Dilemma of "Double-Consciousness": Toni Morrison's Novels* (Athens: The University of Georgia Press, 1995), 24, 29, 69; Terry Otten, *The Crime of Innocence in the Fiction of Toni Morrison* (Columbia,: University of Missouri Press, 1989), 12, 13.

15. Cynthia Davis, "Self, Society, and Myth in Toni Morrison's Fiction," in *Modern Critical View: Toni Morrison,* (ed. Harold Bloom; New York: Chelsea House, 1990), 7.

16. See Cheryl A. Kirk-Duggan, *Misbegotten Anguish: A Theology and Ethics of Violence* (St. Louis: Chalice Press, 2001).

17. Sometimes forensic scientists are known as bone detectives when they

have to find bodies or make identifications when death has occurred so long ago that the body is reduced to a skeleton.

18. Available at Grimm's Fairy Tales at All Family Resources. Online: http://www.familymanagement.com/literacy/grimms/grimms12.html.

19. A. S. Byatt, "Introduction," in Jacob and Wilhelm Grimm, *The Annotated Brothers Grimm*, with Preface and Notes by Maria Tatar (New York: W.W. Norton, 2004), xxviii-xxix.

20. Ibid., xxx-xlv.

21. "Glossary. " *International Information Programs*. Online: usinfo.state.gov/products/pubs/oal/gloss.htm.

22. Jonathan Demme, *The Silence of the Lambs*, MGM, 1991; Thomas Harris, *The Silence of the Lambs* (New York: St. Martin's Press, Reprint edition, 1999).

23. *The Silence of the Lambs* won Academy Awards for Best Picture; Best Director—Jonathan Demme; Best Actor—Anthony Hopkins; Best Actress—Jodie Foster; and Best Adapted Screenplay—Ted Tally.

24. James Berardinelli, "The Silence of the Lambs: A Film Review." Online: http://movie-reviews.colossus.net.

25. Ibid: One night at the family ranch, she awoke and heard lambs screaming, while being slaughtered. Starling tried to save one by carrying it away. She was soon caught and the lamb returned to slaughter. Lecter asks if she can still hear the lambs crying and wonders if she imagines that saving Catherine Martin will finally give her some peace.

26. Alexa Smith, "Not Just Fun and Games," *Presbyterians Today*. Cover story, January/February 2006. Online: http://www.pcusa.org/today/cover/2006/cover0106.htm.

27. "Grand Theft Auto: San Andreas." Online: http://www.rockstargames.com/sanandreas.

28. Ibid.

29. "Grand Theft Auto: Vice City." Online: http://www.rockstargames.com/vicecity/.

30. Smith, "Not Just Fun and Games."

31. Ibid.

4. VIOLENCE AND SYSTEMATIC THEOLOGY

1. See Inna Jane Ray, "The Atonement Muddle: An Historical Analysis and Clarification of a Salvation Theory," ed. Cheryl Kirk-Duggan, *The Journal of Women and Religion*, Vol. 15 (1997).

2. Delores Williams, *Sisters of the Wilderness: The Challenge of Womanist God-Talk* (Maryknoll, N.Y.: Orbis, 1993).

3. Karen Baker-Fletcher, *Dancing with God: The Trinity from a Womanist Perspective*, (St. Louis, Mo.: Chalice Press, 2006), 98-103.

4. Alan Richardson and Alan Bowden, eds., *The Westminster Dictionary of Christian Theology* (Philadelphia: Westminster Press, 1983), s.v. John Hick and

David Hume, "The Problem of Evil": *Dialogues Concerning Natural Religion* (ed. H. D. Aiken; New York: Harper, 1948), 66. *Non-being* claims only one principle of ultimate being or power exists, thus evil is non-existent or imaginary. *Despotism*, tyrannical rule, distances God and denies the existence of evil. *Dualism* claims a good God and evil are equal. *Moral theory* limits God's power. These theories either negate evil or limit God. Other scholars see the question as a matter of logic, evidence, cognitive theocentrism, and unanswered questions or constructive theory. The "Unanswered Question" argument develops when believers need a logical reason for why God allows evil's existence, assuming God allows bad things to happen without knowing why.

5. Joseph A. Komonchak, Mary Collins, and Dermont Lane, eds., *The New Dictionary of Theology* (Wilmington, Del.: Michael Glazier, 1987), s.v. "Problem of Evil," by T. W. Tilley.

6. Komonchak, et al., "Problem of Evil," by Tilley; Kenneth Surin, *Theology and the Problem of Evil* (New York: Basil Blackwell, 1986), 2, 8; Mircea Eliade, *The Encyclopedia of Religion* (New York: Macmillan, 1987), s.v. "Theodicy," by Ronald M. Green; John Hick, *Evil and the God of Love*, revised (San Francisco: Harper & Row, 1977), viii.

7. Hick, *Evil and the God of Love*, 170-92.

8. Ibid., 53-63; Albert Outler, ed., *Augustine: Confessions and Enchiridion*, *The Library of Christian Classics* (Philadelphia: The Westminster Press, 1955), *Confessions*, Bk. 7, chap. 3-5, 12-16, *Enchiridion*, chap. 3-5; Augustine, *The City of God* in *Basic Writings of Saint Augustine* (ed. Whitney J. Oates; Grand Rapids: Baker Book House, 1948), Bk. 11, chap. 16-18; Bk. 12, chap. 1-9.

9. Hick, *Evil and the God*, 211.

10. Irenaeus, *Against Heresies*, V.vi.1; IV.xxxviii.2; IV.xxxix.1; IV.xxxviii.2.

11. Hick, *Evil and the God of Love*, 254-56, 261. Teilhard de Chardin seems to follow this path also.

12. Kenneth Surin, *Theology and the Problem of Evil* (Oxford: Basil Blackwell, 1986), 2-3.

13. See Cheryl A. Kirk-Duggan, *Exorcizing Evil: A Womanist Perspective on the Spirituals* (Maryknoll, N.Y.: Orbis, 1997).

14. Howard Thurman, *The Search for Common Ground: An Inquiry into the Basis of Man's Experience of Community* (New York: Harper and Row, 1971); Walter E. Fluker, *They Looked for a City: A Comparative Analysis of the Ideal of Community in the Thought of Howard Thurman and Martin Luther King, Jr.* (Lanham, Md.: University Press of America, 1989), 3, 29. Thurman was an educator, writer, minister, social prophet, mystic, and visionary.

15. Thurman, *Search for Common Ground*, 4; Howard Thurman, "Community and the Will of God," Mendenhall Lectures, De Pauw University, February 1961, Thurman Papers, Boston University; Howard Thurman, *Deep Is the Hunger* (New York: Harper and Bros., 1951), 64; Howard Thurman, *The Creative Encounter* (New York: Harper and Row, 1954; Richmond Publishers, 1972), 37-38, 53-54, 66.

16. Howard Thurman, *Disciplines of the Spirit* (New York: Harper and Row, 1963; Richmond, Ind.: Friends United Press, 1973), 66; Howard Thurman, "Freedom Under God," Second Century Convocation, Washington University, February 1955, Thurman Papers, Special Collections, Mugar Memorial Library, Boston University; Thurman, *Deep Is the Hunger,* 27; Howard Thurman, *With Head and Heart: The Autobiography of Howard Thurman* (New York: Harcourt Brace Jovanovich, 1979), 134, 268; Fluker, *They Looked for a City,* 49-52.

17. Howard Thurman, *The Luminous Darkness: A Personal Interpretation of the Anatomy of Segregation and the Ground of Hope* (New York: Harper and Row, 1965), 5-12; Howard Thurman, "What Can I Believe In?" *The Journal of Religion and Health* 12 (November 1972): 111-19; Howard Thurman, *The Inward Journey* (New York: Harper and Row, 1961), 105.

18. Kenneth Smith and Ira Zepp, Jr., *Search for the Beloved Community: The Thinking of Martin Luther King, Jr.* (Valley Forge: Judson Press, 1974), 119-40; Fluker, *They Looked for a City,* 81, 90-91, 107.

19. Martin Luther King, Jr., *A Strength to Love* (Philadelphia: Fortress Press, 1981), 110; King, *Where Do We Go,* 171-72.

20. Martin Luther King, Jr., "Nonviolence: The Only Road to Freedom," in James M. Washington, ed., *A Testament of Hope: The Essential Writings of Martin Luther King, Jr.* (San Francisco: Harper and Row, 1986), 54-61.

21. "Black Theology" refers to theology derived from the Black experience, and focuses on racism as the evil. In contrast, "Eurocentric ('white') Theology" is derived from a common Greek and Roman tradition and experience.

22. Deane William Ferm, *Contemporary American Theologies: A Critical Survey,* revised (San Francisco: Harper & Row, 1981, 1990), 44; James H. Cone, *Black Theology & Black Power* (San Francisco: Harper & Row, 1969, 1989), 1, 6-7.

23. Cone, *Black Theology,* 13-29.

24. Ibid., 34-61, 117; James H. Cone, *The Spirituals and the Blues: An Interpretation* (New York: Seabury, 1972), 5-7, 16-19.

25. See Howard Thurman, *Deep River and The Negro Spirituals Speak of Life and Death* (Richmond, Ind.: Friends United Press, 1973); James Cone, *The Spirituals and the Blues.*

26. Alice Walker coined the word *womanist* from the term *womanish,* used by Black mothers to tell their daughters not to act to grown before their time; a Womanist is courageous, in charge, loves and commits to the wholeness and survival of all people. Womanist scholars use this term as a forum to talk about the oppression experienced by poor Black women: sexism, racism, classism. See Alice Walker, *In Search of Our Mothers' Gardens: Womanist Prose* (San Francisco: Harcourt Brace Jovanovich, 1981).

27. Kelly Delaine Brown-Douglas, "Womanist Theology: What Is Its Relationship to Black Theology?" in *Black Theology: A Documentary History,* Vol. II: 1980-1992, (ed. James Cone and Gayraud Wilmore; Maryknoll; N.Y.: Orbis Press), 291-92.